THE BAROMETER OF MODERN REASON

ODÉON

JOSUÉ V. HARARI AND VINCENT DESCOMBES
General Editors

The Barometer of Modern Reason

On the Philosophies of Current Events

VINCENT DESCOMBES

Translated by
Stephen Adam Schwartz

New York   Oxford
OXFORD UNIVERSITY PRESS
1993

Oxford University Press

Oxford   New York   Toronto
Delhi   Bombay   Calcutta   Madras   Karachi
Kuala Lumpur   Singapore   Hong Kong   Tokyo
Nairobi   Dar es Salaam   Cape Town
Melbourne   Auckland   Madrid

and associated companies in
Berlin   Ibadan

Published by Oxford University Press, Inc.,
200 Madison Avenue, New York, New York 10016

Library of Congress Cataloging-in-Publication Data
Descombes, Vincent.
The barometer of modern reason : on the philosophies of current
events / Vincent Descombes ; translated by Stephen Adam Schwartz.
p. cm.—(Odéon) Translated from French. Includes index.
ISBN 0-19-506681-2
ISBN 0-19-507990-6 (pbk)
1. Philosophy, Modern—20th century.
2. Methodology—History—20th century.   I. Title.
B804.D43   1993   190'.9'04—dc20
92-14531

1 3 5 7 9 8 6 4 2

Printed in the United States of America
on acid-free paper

Contents

A Note on the Translation

This translation differs slightly from the original French edition of the text. I consulted with Professor Descombes regularly during the course of translating the book and he graciously offered to augment or slightly revise several passages in order to make them clearer to an English-speaking readership. I owe him a debt of gratitude for this and other suggestions, all of which greatly improved the translation. He and Professor Josué Harari also have my thanks for offering me the project in the first place. David Hasen was very generous in helping me with translations from German. Any remaining infelicities or obscurities are, of course, entirely my responsibility.

The reader should be aware that the French edition of this book was published in 1988, well before the recent historic changes in the Eastern bloc.

Decatur, Ga.   S.A.S.
June 1992

Preface

In an attack on the ideas about poetry prevalent in his time, Charles Baudelaire wrote: "The wind of the century is reaching lunatic force; the barometer of modern reason reads: 'stormy weather.' "[1] It will be said that this assessment is too much at odds with the weather forecast that a progressive mind might offer: the century is drifting toward Enlightenment, the barometer of modern reason reads "clear skies" for the next thousand years.

Baudelaire at least had his poet's barometer, and he based his judgment on what were, to his way of thinking, the modern errors of attributing poetry to the heart, to passion, and to sentiment (rather than to imagination, as one should). But what happens when philosophers are the ones making prognostications about which way the wind of our age is blowing and the likelihood of inclement weather?

My intention in the present book is not to join the ranks of those who have offered readings of the signs of the times. Instead I hope to question the philosophers of the present about their conceptual resources. Where did they find the barometer they use when they speak of "modern reason" or the "spirit of the age"?

---

1. Charles Baudelaire, "Théophile Gautier," in *Selected Writings on Art and Artists*, trans. P. E. Charvet (Cambridge: Cambridge University Press, 1972), p. 269 [translation modified].

It seemed to me that one could set two intellectual projects in opposition. The first rightfully appears to have been a dead end: the project of a metaphysics of the present or of an epochal thinking. The second, I believe, is endowed with a more solid philosophical basis and a clearer signification: the project of an anthropology of modernity.

THE BAROMETER OF MODERN REASON

=1=
Up-to-Date Philosophy

"Reading the morning paper is a kind of realistic morning prayer."[1] This remark by Hegel is often cited to illustrate how interests have changed in the modern age: our gaze has turned away from the invisible beyond and toward daily events. Today, as in the past, no sensible person would think of taking on the business of the day without having prepared himself properly through a spiritual exercise. To start the day off right, it is important to spend a few minutes contemplating what is most crucial. Modern man's sole orison consists in reading the morning paper; for, being a realist, he deems the news to be the first object worthy of his attention at the moment when that attention is sharpest.

Hegel's aphorism suggests that there is a spiritual attitude evident in the predilections of avid newspaper readers. Every morning businessmen, congressmen, high-ranking civil servants, and above all editorialists must ready themselves for the day ahead by reorienting themselves in light of what is. There is thus not as great a difference as one might think between the energetic, enterprising, ambitious, and news-hungry man of action who is so skilled in assessing realities, and the

---

1. G. W. F. Hegel, "Aphorismen aus der Jenenser Zeit," no. 31, in *Dokumente zu Hegels Entwicklung*, ed. Johannes Hoffmeister, 2nd ed. (1936; rpt. Stuttgart-Bad Cannstatt: Frommann, 1974), p. 360.

meditative or contemplative man—the cleric—whose reading is strictly nontopical. What they have in common is that they both start the day with an exercise in meditation. If the exercise is "idealistic," it is called morning prayer. If it is "realistic," it is called reading the paper. In either case the exercise is a means of preparing oneself to live the hours ahead in the frame of mind imposed by the one force that, in the end, decides everything—in the one case, Providence; in the other, the Event.

Reading the newspaper as a kind of spiritual exercise is not to be confused with reading it for diversion. The latter is a way of being well informed, of taking an interest in what is happening, but of doing so from a distance and momentarily, with consequences that are no more serious for the reader than a brief outburst of human feeling, whether of sympathy or indignation. It is in this manner that Mme Verdurin exclaims "How horrible!" upon reading a story on the sinking of the *Lusitania*. Yet, Proust tells us, the news does not discourage her from dipping a croissant into her café au lait, and the taste of the croissant, such a rare delicacy at the time, so outmatches the tragedy of the event that "the expression which spread over her face . . . was in fact one of sweet satisfaction."[2]

The man who practices realistic prayer is a modern individual inso-far as he does not simply stand there amid the things he finds around him but rather arranges them in his mind under the rubric of *current events*. The newspaper aims to report everything of note that has occurred between yesterday and today. In this it reflects the idea that there exists, at every instant, a certain state of the world, and that this state of the world consists of yesterday's state of the world modified by various facts and gestures that have sprung up in the interim. Whether he is serious or frivolous, the newspaper reader equates world events with those facts that have captured the public's attention. Yet in order for the day's events to be surveyed in this manner, they must first be kept at a distance. For the newspaper reader, the noise of the world takes the form of a text, and to read this text one must first have found some kind of provisional refuge. Thus every reader, even the most

---

2. Marcel Proust, *Time Regained*, vol. 3 of *Remembrance of Things Past*, trans. C. K. Scott Moncrieff, Terence Kilmartin, and Andreas Mayor (New York: Random House, 1981), p. 797 [translation modified].

resolutely realistic, risks ending up in the position of a dowager like Mme Verdurin. For time spent reading the newspaper is, by definition, time away from the hustle and bustle of the world. Reading the newspaper requires, for at least an instant, that all commotion quiet down, that all callers stop soliciting, that all emergencies be suspended, and that the overall scene come to a halt. Any one of the incidents reported in the newspaper would disturb the act of reading it, if it were to occur too close to home. Catching up on the news supposes, paradoxically, that nothing too newsworthy has happened nearby. We will not be able to focus our attention on the news, in the way that we do while reading the daily paper, if we find ourselves directly involved in an actual incident that will be in all the headlines tomorrow. That is why the image of Mme Verdurin holding her *Figaro* in one hand, because her other hand must be free for dunking her croissant, provides an indispensable complement to Hegel's aphorism. For Hegel's glorified modern individual, reading the newspaper is a means of preparing oneself to take on the tasks of the day. The realist is a realist because he seeks to show that he is up to his vocation of self-realization *in the world*, that is, in the only arena that really matters. There are, however, other readers who are just as modern and for whom reading the paper is more like a "morning treat," a stimulant that serves to re-awaken their appetite for living by evoking "all the world's misery" and transmuting "all the misfortunes and cataclysms of the universe . . . for the personal use of those of us who are not affected."[3] After all, reading the newspaper is a comfortable way to take note of the latest news; as such, the practice always verges on seeming frivolous and in bad faith, even when it is carried out as resolutely as Hegel would have it. The very conditions of the act are such that the person who takes the time to read the newspaper thereby demonstrates that he considers himself momentarily safe. This tranquillity of the reader is never so striking as when the paper he is holding announces his own misfortune. In old newsreels from just before the war, one can see people anxiously reading a paper hot off the presses. In these scenes of still-intact European cities, where the sidewalks are well lit and the

---

3. Marcel Proust, "Sentiments filiaux d'un parricide," in *Contre Sainte-Beuve*, ed. Pierre Clarac (Paris: Gallimard, 1971), p. 154.

scenery exhibits all the amenities of a well-regulated civilization, every-thing seems too normal and unreal to us, for we know what lies ahead. Men in civilian clothes, women dressed to go out, and ordinary pass-ersby are frozen in place, reading a paper on which something like this is printed: the ultimatum has been delivered; the troops are moving toward the borders; war is inevitable. In these scenes the peace reign-ing in the city has so far been disturbed only by the presence of the words in the banner headline.

Proust provides this rectification of Hegel's aphorism: one can al-ways find someone more "realistic" than oneself. Hegel's modern reader would come across as a staunch realist, were one to compare him, for example, to a Benedictine monk. He might even express himself in quasi-philosophical terms: "All that I believe in," he would say, "are positive things, things that I can touch and do something with." Yet, however realistic he may be, this reader looks like an inveterate idealist to someone who has reached an even more ad-vanced stage of realism—someone who measures reality according to what is actually present and within arm's reach (the cup of coffee in which to dunk a croissant, the newspaper to keep one's mind busy), and who finds the reality of distant events much less pressing because they are invisible for the moment and have no discernible effect on what is happening here and now. A Mme Verdurin, suddenly con-verted to Hegelianism after attending Alexandre Kojève's first semi-nars, might put it this way: "all that I believe in is what seems real *for me, here and now*: this coffee, this newspaper."

There is a lesson in this: for every human attitude imaginable, one can find a corresponding metaphysics. For example, someone is reading his newspaper as earnestly as he can, as if his life depended on it. We ascribe to him an ontology of the historical event: what is real is what changes something in the historical course of things. A woman of leisure is reading her newspaper frivolously. We ascribe to her a solipsistic meta-physics: all this is horrible, but I can just turn the page to change the subject. Thus all the different ways of reading the newspaper—inasmuch as they represent different ways of marking one's order of priorities with regard to what exists—become philosophies in action.

But do we really want to ascribe a metaphysics to Mme Verdurin? Is it we who are slipping philosophy into such unspeculative heads, or is it already there, in an implicit and unformulated state? We may very well be in a position to declare the philosophical meaning of virtually any behavior. Better still, we can rewrite the difference among various human attitudes as a philosophical difference and thereby turn it into a dispute among metaphysicians. The disadvantage, however, in finding depth in ordinary acts—drinking coffee, reading the newspaper, keeping informed—is that it may prove too successful. If there is an entire metaphysics in one's way of drinking coffee, what prevents us from replacing metaphysical meditation with coffee drinking? We run the risk here of forgetting philosophy's golden rule: a philosophy may be "idealistic" or "realistic," dialectical or illuminative, but it cannot allow itself the luxury of not being *difficult*. Who would care about philosophical problems if they were not especially difficult? It is altogether too easy to ascribe a metaphysics to anyone caught up in the ordinary execution of one of his daily chores. And even though one might need a short treatise in ontology to explain someone's behavior fully, he would not need to consult such a treatise in order to decide how to behave. It is we philosophers who will marshal the ontological notions we need in order to talk about that person's way of doing things. This difference must be taken seriously. Moreover, even if it could be proven that there would be no realistic newspaper readers in a culture that had no ontological treatises, we should keep in mind that reading one's newspaper requires no familiarity with such treatises. More likely, the realistic newspaper reader would have trouble understanding how anyone could possibly feel compelled to write a metaphysics.

We can draw the same lesson by looking at the question from a different angle. When we undertake to analyze the practice of reading the morning paper, clearly the best method to follow is to compare it with another morning ritual. We observe that people who read the newspaper no longer remember to say their prayers, whereas people who are committed to praying would not think of plunging into the newspaper before all else. Some exemplary human attitudes are revealed in the process, attitudes that the philosopher calls "realism" and "idealism," respectively. But he would be going too far if he concluded from this that every practice, every custom, and every way of doing and thinking can and should be traced back to a first philosophical principle. Since the eighteenth century, the French language has had a term to describe such abuse of philosophy: a person who misapplies philosophy is a *philosophiste*. Generally speaking, a philosophist is anyone who thinks that he can use philosophy to resolve a difficulty that really ought to be handled differently. It would certainly be philosophistical, for example, to assert that the difference between the culture of prayer and the culture of the newspaper can be reduced to the difference between idealism and realism. Of course, accusing someone of philosophism is a delicate matter. Every philosopher, even the most careful, would look like a philosophist in the eyes of those who think that philosophy itself is unnecessary. Unless one believes there are specific questions that call for a properly philosophical approach, one is apt to denounce the very idea of establishing a difference between "general views" and philosophical theses as arrogant and intolerable. However, the seriousness of philosophy is not to be decided through a choice between *all* and *nothing*. Unimpeachable philosophers like Aristotle tell us that we should not try to establish everything on the basis of philosophy: that would be lacking in *paideia*.[4] The philosophist is free to take this remark as evidence of Aristotle's dogmatism or precritical naiveté. I prefer to see it as proof that one can attach the greatest importance to philosophical analyses without being obliged to say that everything can be reduced to them. For we would truly know very little about the modern epoch, if all we were told about it was that it had proven to be "realistic." The mere idea that a period has become realistic does not tell us whether people read the newspaper with the realism of an achiever or with the realism of a socialite. One is just as likely to "deduce" Napoleon as Mme Verdurin from this metaphysical principle of modernity.

This brings me to the question at the heart of this book: how can philosophy deal with world events [*l'actualité*]?[5]

---

4. Aristotle, *Metaphysics*, IV, 1006^{a}5–7.

5. Translator's note: The French word *actualité* refers not only to what is actual but above all to what is current or present. I have translated this word variously as "current events," "world events," or "the present," depending on the context. On a few occasions where the French word's entire constellation of meanings is implied, I have chosen to leave it untranslated.

Philosophers read the newspaper, too. They do not refrain from writing in it, if asked to do so. And as we are constantly reminded, a "philosophical discourse of modernity" always accompanies the modern individual's investment of interest in what is happening *here and now*. In other words, the modern philosopher's morning prayer will inevitably be realistic. Yet reading the newspaper is no closer to doing philosophy than praying is.

The idea that we must henceforth view philosophy as a "discourse of modernity" was broached in particularly striking fashion by Michel Foucault in his 1983 course on the Enlightenment.[6] There he explained that, as of the eighteenth century, philosophy ceases to concern itself with establishing a link between that which will depart this world, and something else that will remain. Philosophy becomes modern by renouncing the effort to ground the transitory in the eternal. It now turns toward the present, toward the "now." "What," Foucault asks, "is this 'now' that we all inhabit, and that defines the moment in which I am writing?"[7] In this view the philosophical question par excellence is now the question of our present historical being. For to say that philosophy is a "discourse of and on modernity" amounts to saying that it has embraced this question as its essential concern. In other words, the philosopher's "discourse" should bear on things to be found in the newspaper—and not in just any newspaper, but in *today*'s edition. Philosophy is a "discourse of modernity" because it has become, in a sense that is by no means derogatory, a journalistic activity. I do not mean to suggest that the activity of philosophers who think in this way necessarily consists of writing articles for the newspaper. The fact that philosophers write in the paper on subjects of topical interest is not insignificant, yet it is merely the consequence of a mode of thinking whose real importance lies elsewhere. There is more to this view than simply believing that, among the subjects of interest to the philosopher, certain ones might alter our understanding of world events. No, the thesis is even stronger: everything the philosopher has to say touches upon current events.

---

6. Michel Foucault, "Kant on Enlightenment and Revolution," trans. Colin Gordon, *Economy and Society* 15:1 (1986): 88–96.

7. Ibid., p. 88 [translation modified].

Thus Foucault contrasts two "critical traditions" derived from Kant between which, he says, philosophy has been divided. The first is the neo-Kantian tradition of epistemology, which asserts that philosophy should reflect on the conditions of science. The other tradition, to which Foucault himself claims to subscribe, is the tradition of reflecting on our history through questions like "What is our *actualité?*" According to Foucault, this tradition is exemplified by illustrious figures like Hegel, Nietzsche, Weber, and the Frankfurt Marxists. Such a philosophy proposes to offer what Foucault calls variously an "ontology of the present," an "ontology of ourselves," or an "ontology of *actualité.*"

This entire sketch of modern philosophy is, in fact, remarkably in tune with the implications of our Hegelian aphorism. There is, however, one thing that Hegel's saying fails to tell us. When the philosopher opens his newspaper to catch up on the news like everyone else, does he glean something more from it than do other readers? Does he discern a meaning in events that escapes the unilaterally realist public? To put it another way, does he as a philosopher have access to special insights into the news, insights of which even he was unaware before picking up his daily paper?

In short, how can a philosophy purport to be the discourse of our present situation, our *modernity*? This question requires two qualifications in order to rule out any overly trivial responses. First of all, it should be the philosopher who does the talking, and not the citizen that this philosopher also happens to be. What is the philosopher able to say about the news in the name of *philosophy*, and not just in consequence of the opinions that he, like everyone else, may have on current events? We are thereby also asking what it is that justifies presenting an opinion on the contents of today's paper as one that is philosophically articulated and motivated. In other words, we want the philosopher to speak solely in his capacity as philosopher.

Second, the philosopher should speak about world events as constituted by the main headlines of the day's paper. For it is obviously not surprising to find that the philosopher is willing to talk about the news (or any topic, for that matter) in a *reduplicative manner*. That, however, is not what we expect from him here. Certainly, it is the philosopher's job to talk about events considered *as* events, of the present *as* present, and of being *as* being. The move to a reduplicative consideration of things is undeniably philosophical. Thus when the metaphysician has something to say about world events, he always means world events *as* world events—in other words, he seeks to clarify the difference between the "actual" and other modalities of being like the "possible," the "imminent," the "eventual," and the "ideal." These differences belong to metaphysics, or, if you will, to the domain of philosophical grammar. They are equally valid for every edition of the newspaper and have nothing to say that concerns one day's events more than another's. However, the object of a philosophical commentary should not lie in establishing the difference between "the government was overthrown" and other forms like "the government may have been overthrown" and "the government is in danger of being overthrown." Rather, such commentary must take as its object a meaning that can be philosophically culled from the fact that, for example, the government has indeed been overthrown. In other words, it should bear not upon an example, as in the preceding phrases, but upon a historical fact taken from the events of the day.

If there is to be a philosopher of the present state of affairs, he should be neither mere intellectual nor pure metaphysician. The term "intellectual" may be taken to refer to anyone who, while reading the newspaper, is moved to discuss its contents (news and opinions) by invoking not just factual reasoning, but quasi-philosophical reasoning as well. A factual reason supports an argument constructed on the basis of information that is also drawn from the newspaper, whether it be the same paper, yesterday's edition, or a rival tabloid. In this kind of argument, one reacts to what one has just read in the paper with comments of the sort: "This article is mistaken in saying that our side is weaker because, while it may be true that they outnumber us, we are better prepared and better equipped." By contrast, a reason is (almost) philosophical if it is presented as a great general principle to be heeded, such as: might does not make right, you cannot get something for nothing, there is no effect without a cause, etcetera. One might ask why I call these principles quasi-philosophical and not fully philosophical. For they do, in fact, look just like those invoked in the arguments of professional philosophers. Perhaps it might be better to say that philosophy exists anywhere that principles of this sort play a role—in which case one would have to distinguish between "full-time philoso-phers" and "occasional philosophers."

However, the fact that we find exactly the same expression in a variety of discourses does not tell us anything about what role that expression plays in each of them. To determine this, we must decide whether or not the general axiom invoked functions as a philosophical principle. What is philosophical in one context may be merely ideologi-cal in another. This instability is substantially similar to that which Jean Paulhan analyzed in *Les fleurs de Tarbes*: one person's highly original idea is someone else's cliché. Nothing in the disputed expres-sion itself indicates whether it is a deplorable platitude or a richly meaningful invention. This is the dilemma faced by Paulhan's abbé de Saint-Pierre, who had succeeded in distilling all his wisdom into a single notion—that one should never assent to anything that exceeds the limits of one's present judgment: "this is good, for me, for the present." As a result, "when someone kidded him one day about his dictum, he exclaimed: 'Fool! A dictum! This is a truth that took me thirty years to discover.' "[8] Paulhan's anecdote is a clever contrast of, on the one hand, the miseries of personal language—my *idea* is no more than a *saying* for someone who does not find it striking, and likewise my *saying* might be nothing more than a *cliché*—and on the other hand, the reassuring stability of commonplaces, proverbs, and tried-and-true expressions. Thoughts have a different life in the private reflections of an individual than they do within the culture of a group. The same sentences may appear in both contexts; yet among the public they have neither the same rhetorical force nor the same chances for survival.

One could say that the intellectual uses the axiom as a *proverb*, whereas the philosopher uses it as a *maxim*. An example will illustrate this distinction. One occasionally hears mention of a so-called law of the logic of judgments according to which "you cannot derive an 'ought' from an 'is.' " When this law was posited for the first time, it represented the thinking of a philosopher and those who shared his views. It was the result of a thought process. When philosophers of

---

8. Jean Paulhan, *Les fleurs de Tarbes* (1941), in *Oeuvres,* 5 vols. (Paris: Cercle du livre précieux, 1967), III, 49.

this school invoked the principle by which you cannot derive a "you must" from a "such and such is the case," they called upon a maxim that they had adopted after reflection, one they had taken the time to defend. Today that same "law" has become a part of almost everyone's cultural baggage. It may be quoted as a well-known axiom not just by philosophers, but by jurists, literary critics, and others. The axiom in question is no longer a philosopher's postulate. Rather, it has become a philosophical proverb that people eagerly invoke to back up an opinion in public or to undermine an adversary. For example, one way of attacking a report made up of a descriptive first part, and a second part that recommends a certain line of action, is to say that it is dishonest. "We know," one might argue, "that an 'ought' cannot be derived from an 'is.' Yet this report first gives a description of the situation and then makes recommendations. That must mean that the report has a hidden evaluative premise, and is trying to pass off its author's subjective preference as a factual given."

The philosophical proverbs of a culture are so far from constituting a philosophy that they resist the objections of philosophers themselves remarkably well. These objections are only appreciated by philosophers, and do not diminish the value invested in the axioms that make up the public's quasi-philosophy, which one could also call its ideology. For the force underlying these proverbs is not the force of reflection. Rather, such proverbs get their special status from the fact that they are convenient: thanks to them, we find it easier to coordinate the opinions we hold in common on the most diverse subjects. Philosophers who deal in maxims have only a tenuous hold on those who work with proverbs. Thus logicians have explained a thousand times, but to no end, that logic does not prohibit deriving an "ought" from an "is." Here is a perfectly valid example of such a derivation: this water *is poisoned*, therefore you *ought not to drink it*. The fact mentioned in the premise is an excellent reason to advise against—and even, if one has the authority, to prohibit—drinking this water.[9] Yet the proverb in question still holds sway.

_____

9. We normally accept the sentence "This water is poisoned" as an excellent *reason* to pronounce the *prescription* "Do not drink this water." One might object that because this does not hold in all cases, the inference is not valid as such unless one adds a

The philosophical proverbs of an epoch, which can often be traced back to their source in the work of an individual thinker and his followers, form a kind of ideology or philosophical fashion for a particular time. Yet this ideology should not be equated with the theses or dogmatic formulations that can always be given to it, for that would be to transform such proverbs into explicit thoughts. Proverbs are not initially pronounced as propositions and then adopted upon examination. Nor have they been proven to be necessary as hypotheses or presuppositions. Rather, they are already there, agreed upon in advance by everyone. They should not be viewed as containing some merciless code, some secret law that, unbeknownst to all concerned, sets the limits of the thinkable and the unthinkable. An individual can always reject, on his own, the principle that everyone else accepts. This is why the notion of *paradigm* proposed by Thomas Kuhn is useful where Foucault's notion of *épistémè* has proven unworkable. Speaking of a paradigm allows one to say both (1) that there is a social constraint that obliges one to think in accordance with a major model of explanation—the sort of explanation considered to be especially illuminating at the time; and (2) that all those who do not think this way, or who dwell too much on what the preferred mode of explanation does not explain, are temporarily marginalized. In other words, in every epoch there are certain theses that are well received and others that are poorly received—not because the former are better argued

---

premise, which must therefore be "hidden." This premise would say, for example: "You do not want to ruin your health," or "I have been invested with a responsibility for your well-being." This observation is not false, yet it does not undermine the validity of the inference from a logical point of view. *Poisoned water* is *water that ought not to be drunk*. If someone decides to commit suicide, he will try to drink *water that ought not to be drunk*. Thus instead of saying that the inference is not valid according to correct logic, one should say that the conclusion does not yet have the practical value of a decision, unless one attributes a desire to the subject involved in the action. Now there exists *no* practical reasoning that can, in and of itself, have such a practical value without bringing a desire to bear. (Cf. Aristotle: "the intellect does not appear to produce movement without desire," in *De anima*, III, 433ª23, trans. D. W. Hamlyn [Oxford: Oxford University Press, 1968].) Any reasoning based on unconditional prescription would be idiotic: "You must do this because you must do it." (It is well known that Kant's so-called categorical imperative is only unconditional with regard to "pathological" and "empirical" motivations, and that he quite clearly assumes that free beings have the will to conduct themselves both freely and reasonably.)

than the others, but because they lead in the direction of what is expected, a direction determined by current models of intelligibility.

In his philosophy of history, Hegel organizes the course of the various epochs of human history according to purely conceptual necessities. Indeed, the whole argument of his philosophical history rests upon the fact that there is a concept of freedom. In light of what the word "freedom" must mean, it is logically excluded, for example, that our earliest ancestors were authentically free, or, to take another example, that slave societies did not exist at some point; on the other hand, it is logically guaranteed that humanity "finally" will attain the fullest degree of freedom. In turn, the necessity of understanding the word "freedom" in such a way that a whole philosophy of history can be derived from it is itself a logical consequence of the meanings one must ascribe to concepts like being and nothingness, the immediate and the mediated, the finite and the infinite. By proceeding in this manner, Hegel was able to give the impression of having successfully blended, within the single person of the philosopher of historical reality, two roles that had been incompatible until then: the metaphysician and the intellectual.

Traditionally, the metaphysician looks at nothing but the requirements of the Concept. As the maxim goes, "One should not intrude into the immanent rhythm of the Concept either arbitrarily or with wisdom gained elsewhere: such restraint is itself an essential moment of attention to the Concept."[10] On the other hand, the intellectual's function is precisely to engage in "personal intrusions," to give his opinion, to interrupt the "immanent rhythm of the Concept" in order to suggest other kinds of music. In fact, what interests the intellectual is not the "Concept" and its "immanent rhythm" but rather new ideas, the mood of the public, and the direction in which things are headed.

We should not overlook the innovative aspect of the Hegelian synthesis. Whether it was totally successful or not, this synthesis established an articulation between two genres: an ancient genre of specula-

---

10. G. W. F. Hegel, "Preface to *The Phenomenology of Spirit*," in *Hegel: Texts and Commentary*, ed. and trans. Walter Kaufmann (Notre Dame, Ind.: University of Notre Dame Press, 1977), p. 88.

tion that can be found in Plato's *Parmenides* or in the treatises of Proclus; and a recent genre of intellectual life whose main representatives in France were given the name of "Philosophes." Before Hegel, *either* one published speculative systems *or* (an exclusive disjunction) one wrote in gazettes. The philosopher trained as a Hegelian aspires to write a speculative system *and* to take part in the formation of public opinion. Moreover, these two activities should not remain separated: the System is what dictates the article to be published in the newspaper. These are the components of the typical career of a young Hegelian intellectual: working at night on his System, and then capitalizing on it during the day in his public pronouncements.

It goes without saying that philosophy as the French understood it during the century of the Enlightenment represents the most extreme rejection of the speculative constructions that had been put forth from Plato to Malebranche. As we know, the language of the eighteenth century designates someone as a "Philosopher" in virtue of his opinions and state of mind, rather than his adherence to a specific discipline of thought. In fact, the Philosophes did quite well without philosophy. As the historian Carl Becker comments, "There is one not unimportant point about the Philosophers that ought, in simple fairness to them, to be noted in passing, especially since few writers take the trouble to mention it: the Philosophers were not philosophers."[11] It is undoubtedly for this reason that a capital letter is commonly used to differentiate this meaning of the word: one is referring not to a profession, but to a human type. One speaks of the Philosopher as one speaks of the Danube Peasant, the noble savage, or Punchinello. A Philosopher is anyone who possesses the virtues required for participating in a circle of thinkers: tolerance, a critical mindset, politeness, lack of prejudices, and so on.

But for the citizens of the Republic of Letters, the Hegelian philosopher is an unexpected companion. Like them, he is preoccupied by current events. Yet he speaks about them in astonishing terms. He is heard describing the state of the world in an esoteric style reminiscent of some secret society: "the spiritual dawn of presence," "the recollec-

---

11. Carl Becker, *The Heavenly City of the Eighteenth-Century Philosophers* (New Haven, Conn.: Yale University Press, 1932), p. 34.

tion and Calvary of the absolute spirit."[12] What a French Philosophe would find most difficult to accept in Hegel is his method. The idea that one must reel off in advance, and in their necessary order, all the concepts that make up the logical structure of the world, and then use them as a grid for judging and pronouncing what is "real" and well founded in being, versus what is mere "appearance," an ephemeral existence destined to disappear—this conception of method is diametrically opposed to that of a Philosopher, a fellow who believes himself to be enlightened precisely because he approaches experience *without presuppositions*.

As for whether the Philosophers themselves might not be unwittingly doing something similar to the Hegelian thinker (i.e., adopting in advance a conceptual scheme for interpreting experience), *that* is a different matter. One thing, at least, seems clear: it is because the Hegelian philosopher is armed with a metaphysics that he takes the liberty of speaking about the world situation and not just about possibilities. The intellectual or the Enlightenment Philosopher does not read the newspaper to find out how to judge the news. Rather, he reads the newspaper to know what is happening, and his reason gives him the means of knowing whether or not what is happening marks an advancement for humanity. In other words, his reason tells him *what progress would be*, and the newspaper tells him *whether there is progress* (through the application of the norms of progress provided by reason to the information given in the newspaper). The Hegelian philosopher considers the perspective of the *Aufklärer* to be "unilateral." He might say: "we cannot immediately know *what progress would be*. We must develop a concept of freedom or of the rational." The question for us then becomes one of determining how it is possible for there to be a philosophy of the present, if one eliminates both metaphysics and the abstractly normative reason of the Enlightenment.

One cannot help asking this question when one sees Foucault using the high-flown scholarly word "ontology" to characterize the kind of philosophy that is turned toward the question of the present. He has on occasion formulated the question as follows: "The question of

---

12. G. W. F. Hegel, *Phenomenology of Spirit*, trans. A. V. Miller (Oxford: Oxford University Press, 1977), pp. 111, 493.

philosophy is the question of this present that constitutes us. That is why philosophy today is entirely political and entirely historicist. It is the politics immanent in history, and the history that is indispensable to politics."[13]

One can see quite clearly how someone who undertakes to describe "this present that constitutes us" will end up writing a *history of the present*. It is less clear why he insists on calling it an *ontology of the present*. The technical word "ontology" has never been used to designate anything but conceptual (metaphysical) research. Although this type of research is not obliged to adopt a Hegelian method, the questions asked— whatever the philosophical style—must not be those one would ask in an empirical inquiry or in the course of archival work. An ontology of the present must tell us about the present *as* present, about time *as* time, about the unaccomplished *as* unaccomplished, about the past *as* past. Yet conceptual discussions of this order are notoriously absent from Foucault's writings. In keeping with the positivist program, he can only conceive of studying a concept in the historical mode. Which amounts to saying that an *entirely historicist philosophy* may well be political but, prima facie, it has nothing to do with any sort of ontology.

If there is no difference between the philosophy of the present and the history of the present, it would be clearer to say, along with Richard Rorty, that philosophy is utterly indistinguishable from rhetoric. Or rather, that philosophy is only distinguishable by virtue of a rhetorical difference, a difference in style, but not in validity. To return to the distinction made earlier, this comes down to holding that there really is no difference between the *maxims* of a philosopher and the *proverbs* of a culture. Rhetoric openly acknowledges that it uses "proverbs"—that is, venerable opinions, well-known sayings and commonplaces. These rhetorical premises are only as good as the people who find them persuasive. The philosopher claims that the maxims on which he ultimately settles have a force surpassing that of the proverbs of public opinion. This is the philosophical project of *radical thought*, which consists in

---

13. Michel Foucault, "Power and Sex," trans. David J. Parent, in *Michel Foucault: Politics, Philosophy, Culture*, ed. Lawrence D. Kritzman (New York: Routledge, 1988), p. 121 [translation modified].

thinking without—and eventually against—the proverbs of one's village. Rorty denounces such an ambition as the effect of an illusion. The only way for the radical philosopher to provide a foundation for the premises of his culture is by using the proofs that are accepted in that culture; that is, by using precisely the proofs that presuppose those premises. A desire to distinguish the maxim-philosopher from the proverb-philosopher (or the *philosopher* from the *intellectual*) implies that one believes that philosophy, as opposed to the other liberal arts, can give us a position outside any culture, any tradition, or any particular language. That is tantamount to forgetting "that nothing counts as justification unless by reference to what we already accept, and that there is no way to get outside our beliefs and our language so as to find some test other than coherence."[14] Thus Rorty beckons us to move beyond the conception of philosophy to which Plato, Aristotle, Spinoza, or Hegel subscribed. Under the banner of "pragmatism," he recommends reuniting the sect of philosophers with the overall intellectual community, a suggestion that is in accord with the conception of philosophy espoused by Cicero or the Humanists.

The important point is that philosophy conceived of as the rhetoric of a generation is not radical, is not held to be so, and does not want to be so. This is perhaps the reason that led Foucault to lay claim to the metaphysical word "ontology" at the very moment when he was, in fact, renouncing all autonomous philosophical research.[15] Foucault

---

14. Richard Rorty, *Philosophy and the Mirror of Nature* (Princeton, N.J.: Princeton University Press, 1979), p. 178. I believe that Rorty is not sufficiently attentive to the possibility that by abolishing the difference between philosophy and rhetoric he is also, necessarily, abolishing the difference between the *philosophical* conception of rhetoric (as the art of persuading someone through *arguments* about what is probable and plausible) and the opposing conception of rhetoric, the one used by antiphilosophers for whom the difference between philosophy and elegant, compelling speeches is just a question of *style*. According to this *antiphilosophical* conception, rhetoric is an art of persuasion through *rhetorical flourishes* (extended metaphor, insistent metonymy, etc.) or as one might say today, through the play of the *signifier*. However, the manner in which Rorty composes his own texts shows that he prefers the argumentative rhetoric of the philosophers to the flowery and ornate rhetoric of the antiphilosophers.

15. Others have been better able to characterize the interest of those of Foucault's works meant to constitute a *history of the present*. I do not wish to pass judgment on that history here. But whether it is excellent or implausible, a history of the present is not, could not be, and above all should not be an ontology of the present.

persists in his ambition to think radically. And from philosophy he retains at least this: he wants to be able to look at *our* proverbs as if they belonged to a different culture. But to look at them with such detachment usually means criticizing them.

The critical ambition of Foucault's investigations has been widely remarked. Though it is quite conceivable that historical work might have critical repercussions, it is harder to see how it could lead to *radical* revisions. In fact, a history of the present will establish its criterion for what is modern by contrasting the most advanced and the most backward sectors of the population being studied, with the difference between the "advanced" and the "traditional" being that provided by the population itself. Understood in this sense, "modernity" is a matter of degrees: there are some cities that are more modern than others, techniques that are more modern than others, families that are more modern than others, pedagogies that are more modern than others. The indices used by the historian to detect the modern are unimportant here. Whatever portrait he sketches of modern humanity, the historian's portrait will most certainly not be ontological. It is a historical description of the population in question, and not an ontological determination. Although the difference may seem trivial to those who have no use for ontology, it is nonetheless decisive in assessing the possibility of a philosophy of the present. The historian's depiction of what is modern is so constituted that it may very well be fully applicable to no more than a minority of the population. In this sense, it has a status akin to that of etiquette manuals. Manuals abound on how to be a modern man or modern woman, on the modern young lady, even on modern stimulants.[16] Such essays waver between factual

---

The fact that Foucault's writings contain no autonomous philosophical research strikes me as not only incontestable, but clearly deliberate on his part. It should moreover be noted that the authors who have recently attempted to uncover the philosophy that *he would have written,* had he chosen to reveal it himself, have reached contradictory results. According to Hubert Dreyfus and Paul Rabinow, Foucault was a pragmatic philosopher: see their *Michel Foucault: Beyond Structuralism and Hermeneutics*, 2nd ed. (1982; rpt. Chicago: University of Chicago Press, 1983). According to Gilles Deleuze, he was a transcendental one: see his *Foucault*, trans. Seán Hand (Minneapolis: University of Minnesota Press, 1988).

16. Translator's note: This is an allusion to Honoré de Balzac's *Traité des excitants modernes.*

reporting and satire. They are never too far removed from Flaubert's "dictionary of received ideas," because the way in which the observer of modern mores uses the word "modern" is necessarily related to its ordinary usage. Normally, the word implies something desirable— even enviable. Outside the mainstream it can also be used in a negative sense and as a means of resisting superficial fads. In any case, the important point is that not everyone is obliged to be modern. Further-more, the historian and the sociologist are only interested in modern tendencies because they have assessed the force of conservative ones. Consequently, if someone does not exhibit the putative indices of the "modern," it will not be said that *he does not exist* (or that the pro-posed indices are imprecise), but rather that *he is different*. The critical significance of a history of the present is that it can highlight the nonmodern, or even antimodern, elements of the contemporary epoch, and show that those elements are neither negligible nor moribund. This satirical tenor of a history of the present as Foucault understood it was in fact heralded by the antimodern historian Philippe Ariès.

However, if the history of the present truly had an ontological signifi-cance, one would have to suppose that whatever does not seem to conform to the (ontological) index of the modern *does not exist*, can-not really be, or has only the appearance of presence. Calling philoso-phy an "ontology of the present" implies that we exist *only if* we are present in a modern mode. In "Hegelian" terms this could be taken to mean that the antimodern contingent has no future, that is, that it is a "phenomenon" without any "reality." One might also take it to mean, in "Heideggerian" terms, that would-be antimoderns are prisoners of the modern mode of thinking. One could propose other reductions of this sort. But in each case the word "ontology" must introduce the perspective of reduplication. If ontology pays particular attention to the "present" and the "now," it is so that the decisive reduplication can be performed on present-being, the kind of being that is ours insofar as we exist *now*. Speaking of an *ontology of the present* is a way of announcing that one wants to derive the essential traits of our lives—the traits by which we are, precisely, these modern beings rather than others (or nothing at all)—from the meaning associated with the expression "to be now," by which we therefore denote more than a date, more than a period, namely, a specific mode of being.

Any ontological thesis is necessarily strong. It does not allow for any exception or approximation. We cannot change the fact that all we will ever be will be granted to us in a "now." If, on top of that and in keeping with the "ontology of ourselves," we had to maintain that the physiognomy of our being *is a function* of the fact that this present reality of ourselves is granted to us *now*, we would not have the slightest chance of "being" differently. What I mean to say is, there would not be the slightest chance for certain people to think or act differently from their contemporaries. It would be ontologically established that, once our entire being is reduced to the being of today, we can only "be" in today's mode.

These bizarre consequences show that the metamorphosis of the *history of the present* into an *ontology of the present* is serious business. The term "ontology," as we have seen, introduces the notion of necessity into the chronicle of today's mores. One could even speak figuratively of a destiny. What we are, we were "destined" to be.[17] Yet the very notion of a constraint of this order is necessarily foreign to an authentic history of the present, a history that it is hard to imagine being overly concerned with the meaning of the concept *to be now*, given that such histories are almost exclusively focused on the diversity of what actually is, now.

If the philosopher of the present has the same object of study as the historian of the present—and moreover, the same way of working—it is difficult to see how he can come to conclusions that are properly philosophical. Our problem thus remains intact: what indeed would a philosophy conceived of as a "discourse of and on modernity" be? What is expected of philosophers when they are asked to examine the present?

---

17. Translator's note: This is an allusion to Heidegger's notion of *Geschick,* which in everyday German means "destiny," "fate," or "sending," among other things. In his later philosophy Heidegger uses this term to refer to the original and extra- (or archi-) historical dispensation and ordering of Being, in the light of which beings can appear. Thus *das Seinsgeschick* (the *Geschick* of Being), according to Heidegger, determines what it is possible to do and think in a given epoch. See Martin Heidegger, *The Principle of Reason,* trans. Reginald Lilly (Bloomington, Ind.: Indiana University Press, 1991), pp. 61–62, as well as the translator's introduction, pp. xiv–xv.

=2=

The Philosophy of the French Revolution

—Er ist ein Prinz.
—Mehr! Er ist ein Mensch!
Mozart, *Die Zauberflöte*

A few years ago a collection of French translations of Kant's shorter writings was being prepared for republication as a paperback edition under the title *La philosophie de l'histoire*.[1] Until that time, the book had always been sold under the austere and faded yellow cover used by the Aubier publishing house. For the new edition a more evocative layout was deemed to be in order. As an illustration for the new cover, a stylized figure was settled upon, one evocative of the "Marseillaise" or of beckoning liberty: an indignant matron in Phrygian cap was depicted, shouting what was no doubt some revolutionary slogan. To arouse the interest of those who might be put off by the name "Kant," the following subtitle was printed under the title: *The Origins of Hegel's Thought*. The message is apparently that Kant can be seen as the precursor to the true philosopher of history, Hegel, after which one would presumably move on to Marx. On the back cover is the following blurb:

> Only once, to the great astonishment of his neighbors, who were familiar with his comings and goings, did Kant modify the route of his daily constitutional: that was the day when, at the time of the Revolution, he went to await the arrival of the mail bearing the latest news from France. This anecdote attests to the interest taken

---

1. Immanuel Kant, *La philosophie de l'histoire* (Paris: Denoël-Gonthier, 1980).

by the philosopher from Königsberg in the most important political
event of his time.

This text speaks volumes. A Frenchman finds it perfectly natural to
talk about *the* Revolution. There is no danger that anyone will take
him to be referring to anything other than to *our* Revolution—say, to
the American Revolution. Moreover, no one doubts for an instant that
the Revolution—a major event of the time—was also a major political
development in Königsberg. It seems to go without saying that the
philosophy of history elaborated by Kant in Königsberg should have
the closest of connections with the events of French history. Since we
know that philosophy deals with universal history, it strikes us as
perfectly natural that the center of such universal history—at least in
1789—should be in Paris.

Recently, while France has been approaching the bicentennial of the
taking of the Bastille, these Kantian texts have become the subject of
renewed interest. The reason for this seems clear: it is hoped that these
texts will provide the elements of a philosophy of political judgments
concerning the events of a revolution. The feeling prevails today that
such a philosophy has been sorely lacking during the past few decades.
Particularly in France, the commitment to various revolutionary movements has distinguished itself by its inconsistency and lack of discern-
ment. In this regard, though the cover of the "Médiations" paperback
edition of the Kant anthology meets the expectations of the public by
means of its illustration, its subtitle renders it somewhat dated. What is
today being sought in Kant is rather an *antidote* to Hegel and Marx: a
means of judging events that is not reduced to accepting the *entirety* of
what is glossed over in the word "Revolution." Rightly or wrongly, all
the "dialectical" conceptions of history have been reproached for their
immorality. The infamous Hegelian adages describing universal history
as the last judgment and glorifying the "work of the negative"—
vulgarized into Stalinist parlance as the "impossibility of making an
omelette without breaking eggs"—have proven all too useful to political militants, allowing them to discharge themselves of the hard task of
judging. For too long it has been repeated that history judges men and
that the judgment of history is harsh for those who claim to judge *it*
from any "abstract" or "one-sided" point of view derived from an

isolated principle, that those who would judge history ahistorically will find themselves swept away by it to an immanent hell, charmingly dubbed "the dustbin of history."

The problem posed by any return to Kant is that such returns have been preceded by innumerable passages "von Kant bis Hegel" and "von Hegel zu Nietzsche." Here it is not the history of ideas that is at issue but the very philosophy of those ideas. The new Kantians who present contemporary philosophy with a choice between *Kant or Hegel* do not deny that the formula cited earlier is literally correct: the origins of Hegel's thinking on history are to be sought in Kant. However, this is not to be taken as a statement about historical influences, but merely as indicating that any initiation into the Hegelian conception calls for an exposition of both the areas of validity and the insurmountable difficulties of the Kantian position. Once we are thus initiated, though, if we are subsequently shown the contradictions implied by the Hegelian position, we will presumably break with Hegelianism. But if that implies a return to Kant, don't we run the risk of going in circles? Won't we once again be preoccupied with the paradoxes of Kantianism and the search for a solution to them? Before looking to Kant—the philosopher of human rights—as some kind of archangel who will stand up to the philosophies of the fait accompli, it would be nice to know we are not traveling in a closed circuit wherein the affirmation of principles leads us to seek their realization in a concrete universal, and the flaws of the concrete universal compel us to reaffirm the great principles.

The return to Kant to which we are today being summoned is above all a return to a philosophy of judgment. What makes Kant's view of the French Revolution invaluable is that it is a judgment passed on a contemporary event. It is easy to be wise twenty years after the fact. But we would prefer that philosophy enlighten us during the battle, without our having to wait for the end of hostilities or "the judgment of history." Without such timeliness, our knowledge seems tainted. The contemporary intellectual can easily condemn today the misdeeds of yesterday, in particular the alignment with Stalinism, but as long as he remains satisfied with saying "if I had only known," he has still not begun the indispensable philosophical reform of political judgment. *Of course* we would have avoided committing yesterday's errors, if we had known that their historical victims would reproach us for them today. Yet the problem regarding judgments on contemporary events is not resolved by saying how I would have judged if I had known—or even how I *should have* judged if I had known—but how I *could have* reasonably judged, given the information at my disposal at the time.

It seems to us today that Kant too was familiar with our problem: how should one go about applying timeless principles to situations that we call "events" precisely because they are unprecedented? How are we to apply principles that are supposed to be unconditional to complicated situations in which the right course has not yet been clearly revealed? In Kant one hopes to find the outlines of *the book he never wrote*: a Critique of Political Reason.[2] In the absence of such a Fourth Critique, attention has been directed toward the Third, the *Critique of Judgment*, in which Kant explains how it is possible to derive norms for our judgments of taste (e.g., "this is beautiful") from the very idea of human communication. For though it is in some respects a fact that communication between humans is possible, it is more than a mere fact. The idea of communication also entails certain obligations and constraints. Each time someone addresses someone else, he assumes that communication is possible. Provided that what he says is comprehensible and that his interlocutor agrees to understand it, he will be understood. And his utterance will be comprehensible if it is formulated in such a way as to satisfy the norms of communication. These norms stipulate that the speaker should appeal to his interlocutor's power for reasoning, here defined as the communicative faculty. Kant calls these norms the "maxims of common sense," of which there are three: (1) that one's thought be *unprejudiced* ("think for yourself"); (2) that one's thought be *broadened* ("think from the standpoint of everyone else"); and (3) that one's thought be *consonant* ("always think in a self-consistent way").[3] It is above all the first maxim—the one prescribing the autonomy of reason and the struggle against prejudice—that defines the *Aufklärung* for Kant. This Kantian

2. Jean-François Lyotard, *The Differend: Phrases in Dispute*, trans. Georges Van Den Abbeele (Minneapolis: University of Minnesota Press, 1988), p. 130.

3. Immanuel Kant, *Critique of Judgment*, trans. Werner S. Pluhar (Indianapolis, Ind.: Hackett, 1987), §40.

perspective has been resuscitated by the contemporary partisans of the *Aufklärung*—Eric Weil in France and Jürgen Habermas in Germany—in an attempt to reconstruct rationalist philosophy on the foundation of reason defined as the communicative faculty rather than as the power of each individual to arrive independently at manifest truths.

From these three maxims Kant concludes that aesthetic judgments have a relative legitimacy. Since communication is possible, it is legitimate to suppose that even judgments of taste—which would seem to be irreducibly subjective—can be shared with others. In expressing our aesthetic pleasure, we form a judgment. If it is really a judgment, and not simply an exclamation, such an expression already contains within it the idea that it is possible for our aesthetic opinions to be communicated to others and shared by them. The fact that discussions take place regarding matters of taste shows that each of us is already a citizen of a cosmopolitan republic made up of all those subjects endowed with common sense.

But where is the critique of political reason in all this? Cornelius Castoriadis is right to point out how odd it is to seek Kant's politics in his aesthetics:

> Why should we return to the *Critique of Judgment* when Kant's entire practical philosophy explicitly strives to formulate rules and maxims for judgment and choice in "practical" matters? Why, in recent debate, have the apparently solid bases for fundamental political judgment proposed by Kant been neglected when they have productively inspired neo-Kantian socialists, Austro-Marxists and others for some eighty years?[4]

Such questions are entirely justified. Why is a practical philosophy being sought in Kant's texts on the validity of aesthetic judgments, rather than in his later texts dealing with issues in ethics, philosophy of law, and politics? Apparently we want no part of a simple reaffirmation of republican principles derived from the idea of autonomy. After all, the Hegelian critique of Kant hit its mark. The formulas of the moral law have no automatic applications. Taken by themselves, they are without content. This objection, though "classic" and "familiar,"

---

4. Cornelius Castoriadis, *Domaines de l'homme* (Paris: Seuil, 1986), pp. 270–71.

is nonetheless persuasive. In fact, what we are interested in learning is how to pass judgment on an event. In order to be able to subsume an event under principles like the respect for rights or the demand for autonomy, one must have already described it in one way or another. One has to have decided between competing versions of the same event, and this step goes so much without saying that it tends to be immediately forgotten under the purely abstract formulation. Am I acting in violation of the Law governing vehicular traffic if I drive on the left-hand side of a two-way street in Paris? What if each of us unpredictably decided to do the same? By what right do I make an exception of myself? My maxim is not universalizable! True enough, but am I supposed to run over the workers who are repairing the right-hand side of the roadway, in order to satisfy the entirely reasonable requirement that we drive only on that side of the road? My action is not subject to evaluation as long as it has not been described in one particular way or another. Only "under a description" is an action intentional, as an analytic philosopher following Elizabeth Anscombe might say, and only thus is it subject to the application of normative predicates.[5] Before undertaking the application of grand principles to an event, one must have already decided on a *judicious* version of the event to be, so to speak, "thought." Our real problem is therefore one of knowing what it is to demonstrate judgment with regard to an event. That is, to demonstrate judgment in choosing the terms that allow an appropriate narration of the event.

It so happens that the version of the French Revolution that Kant felt he could discuss philosophically is the aesthetic version. What remains to be seen is whether it is possible to pass political judgment on events described in purely aesthetic terms.

Of the texts making up *La philosophie de l'histoire*, one in particular justifies the supposition that the French Revolution was the focal point for Kant's thinking on the philosophy of history. The text is the second section of "The Contest of the Faculties" (written in 1795), which takes up the question: Is humanity constantly progressing? As one might expect, Kant's approach to this question is epistemological: If there were such progress, how would we know? By way of a re-

---

5. G. E. M. Anscombe, *Intention* (Oxford: Basil Blackwell, 1957).

sponse, he develops a theory of "historical signs," which are more like indicators than hermeneutic oracles. And it is in this context that Kant brings up the French Revolution.

The reader of this text cannot fail to be struck by the emphasis Kant puts on the geographical distance between him (in his capacity as philosopher) and the events in question. He takes pains to underscore that he is writing "in a country more than a hundred miles removed from the scene of the Revolution."[6] In Kant's view, though the French are to be commended for having overthrown their monarchy, the reader should not hasten to conclude that other nations should do the same. Conclusions should not be drawn *here* (in Prussia) on the basis of what the philosopher has to say about the goings-on *over there* (in France). Often Kant is said to have been taking precautions in such texts, adopting a moderate tone in order to avoid censorship. This explanation is flawed, for Kant's entire argument rests on the possibility of clearly distinguishing the "stage" of the Revolution, with its insurgent "actors," from the place of the *public* in whose name the philosopher speaks. Without this distinction between the stage [*la scène*] and the audience [*la salle*], as Lyotard puts it,[7] Kant's reasoning collapses.

For it is not the French Revolution itself that indicates that humanity is progressing. Does the occurrence of the Revolution constitute progress for humanity? It is impossible to tell. But don't the actions taken by the revolutionaries at least prove that men are capable of laying claim to their rights? No one knows this either. Who can say whether the Jacobins are motivated by the idea of Liberty they invoke or by mere self-interest?

Instead, the historical sign of progress is provided by the enthusiastic reaction of the public. It is as though the public is attending a spectacle and considers it as such, neither dangerous nor auspicious for them as spectators. Only in such circumstances have we isolated the infallible sign: the enthusiasm of a public that has nothing to lose or gain in this episode proves that humanity can and must progress.

---

6. Immanuel Kant, "The Contest of the Faculties," in *Political Writings*, ed. Hans Reiss, trans. H. B. Nisbet, 2nd ed. (1970; rpt. Cambridge: Cambridge University Press, 1991), p. 182n.

7. Lyotard, *The Differend*, p. 167.

In order to give a philosophical opinion on the French Revolution, Kant enlists a plethora of precautionary measures that can only discourage readers hoping that this text will provide the model for a critical political philosophy. In essence, what Kant says is this: if we are present at the *representation* of a drama in which the great moral cause of the ancien Régime (honor) and that of the Revolution (human rights) are opposed, we may well be moved by the excellence and nobility of the partisans of honor, but cannot keep ourselves from identifying with the partisans of the Revolution.

> Even the old military aristocracy's concept of honour (which is analogous to enthusiasm) vanished before the arms of those who had fixed their gaze on the *rights* of the people to which they belonged, and who regarded themselves as its protectors. And then the external public of onlookers sympathised with their exaltation, without the slightest intention of actively participating in their affairs.[8]

What better way of saying that the philosopher, as philosopher, has nothing to say about the *event* of the French Revolution? As for the *principles* invoked by the Revolution—that's another story. If one presses him on the subject, the philosopher will ask to be allowed to replace the object of political judgment (the revolutionary event) with an object of philosophical judgment (the right of a people to decide its own fate). And what if one insists that the philosopher take a position on the events at hand, for example, on the fact that the people of a country have just put into place their own constitution (or even *three* constitutions between 1789 and 1795—those of the Constituent Assembly, of the Montagnards, and of Thermidor, respectively)? The philosopher has nothing to tell you that you did not already know or that you would not be better off deciding for yourself: that there are many interests at stake; that though the revolutionary cause is indisputably noble, the defenders of this cause are perhaps not its best advocates; that it is unlikely that the French would again want to go through such an ordeal; that the progress of the Enlightenment generally moves "from the top downward" and not "from the bottom upward"; and so on. As a philosopher, Kant is too highly attuned to

---

8. Kant, "The Contest of the Faculties," p. 183.

the difference between philosophical and empirical propositions to believe it easy for the philosopher to install himself before the play of events and issue a declaration as to their meaning. It is for this reason that he turns his attention to the reaction of the audience instead of observing the events on the stage. In this text, which is so concerned with finding the signs indicative of progress, Kant is focused on the public's *aesthetic* response precisely because he wants to exclude everything that can only be an object for *political judgment*. The reaction of the public proves that there is progress whether the Revolution succeeds or fails. It does not even matter if the Revolution results in atrocities and universal misery, because the only thing that matters here is the disclosure of "the moral disposition of the human race."

Out of all possible versions of the French Revolution he could have evoked, Kant thus takes up the aesthetic one, in which the Revolution is presented as a series of distant events without any repercussions for neighboring countries. Though it is possible that the general European public took such a view of things at the outset, they were mistaken to think that they were out of harm's way simply because they were in Milan, Frankfurt, or Berlin. The spectators who applauded from the rear of the hall were lacking in judgment, for they were blind to the fact that the action could not remain restricted to the stage for very long.

All of which raises the following question: Why must the proof of progress that Kant seeks have any connection to a real event? Why isn't the enthusiasm displayed in a *real* theater at the performance of some exalted drama sufficient for Kant? One thing is certain: Kant's reasoning does not require that the enthused public be well informed about the actual goings-on in France. What arouses the sublime sentiments of the public is only the representation, the revolutionary *idea*. Of course the public wants to believe that its representation of the events is an accurate one. But the public need do no more than sincerely hold this belief to ensure the presence of the historical sign of progress.

The scandalous consequences of any attempt to extract a politics from Kant's observations on the European enthusiasm for the Revolution are immediately obvious. If we expect to make any judgments whatsoever about the Revolution on the basis of the reactions of the public, it is only a matter of time before we members of that *other* public—the "universal" public—find ourselves endorsing all sorts of revolutionary parties whenever hearsay favorably predisposes us to their cause. We have seen the extent to which certain specialists in the support of causes unfamiliar to the public—and often equally unfamiliar to the specialists themselves—have stretched the casuistic art of *directed intention*. "Yes," they say, "I backed Mao and Stalin, but I didn't *intend* my enthusiasm for the flesh-and-blood Stalin or for Mao as the Chinese knew him. What I was supporting was the noble idea of revolution, the glorious image of the proletarian leader, the inspiring figures that Stalin and Mao should have been, had they filled the roles assigned to them in our representation."

Kant's use of the word "enthusiasm," by which he means a sort of sublime feeling, should have alerted us to the danger of lending political significance to a text whose thrust is epistemological. Indeed, the situation arousing such sublime feelings is characterized for Kant by the distance separating the spectator from the spectacle. What is sublime is a violent disturbance of the world, but only on the condition that the observer remain undisturbed. According to Kant's now canonical analysis, sublime spectacles are those that present a concentration or unleashing of violent forces (at least if we stick to the "dynamic" sublime). Just as there is a sublimity to war, so there is a sublimity to the storm and the volcano, and for the same reason. In each case the spectator whom the awesome power threatens to pulverize into dust is also he who, in measuring *its* force, finds an opportunity to take the measure of *his own* forces. For no mere material force can triumph over the resolve of a freely acting will. However, Kant points out that we have the luxury of aesthetically appreciating these exhibitions of man's sublimity only on the condition that we, the observers, are not there on the scene. Someone who stands his ground in the face of limitless might is sublime. Though *he* is the one who demonstrates grandeur, it is we, the comfortably sheltered subjects of the aesthetic experience, who apprehend this greatness. A sailor taken by surprise by a gale or a voyager surrounded by a storm would have to be reckless or inhuman not to be afraid. "Yet the sight of them [cataclysms] becomes all the more attractive the more fearful it is, provided that we are in a safe place. And we like to call these objects sublime because they raise the soul's fortitude above its usual middle range."⁹

As long as one remains within the aesthetic realm, the fact that the subject who experiences human grandeur is in fact sheltered from the danger is irrelevant. Indeed, this fact is constitutive of aesthetic experience as such: one has to be awed by the danger without being imperiled by it. The danger's mere aesthetic presence is sufficient. In any case we are more like tourists than combatants in this confrontation with danger. "This self-estimation loses nothing from the fact that we must find ourselves safe in order to feel this exciting liking; therefore, the fact that the danger is not genuine in no way implies (as it might seem) that the sublimity of our intellectual ability might also not be genuine."¹⁰ It is not necessary that the danger be real precisely because we are dealing with aesthetics—that is to say, with a *play* of possibilities. Each time that there is a tempest, we *could* be at sea rather than in security on the beach. We can even imagine that we *are* out there, and by means of this fantasy we can immediately experience exactly what we would feel if we actually were at sea. It is then that we understand how frightened we would be: that we would probably be overpowered, but not necessarily humiliated.

But it would be pure sophistry to allow oneself to surreptitiously slide from playing with the possibility of danger to taking the danger seriously, treating the spectacle of the tempest as though it were a real tempest. The aesthetic experience provides an opportunity to take sight of our *destination*, of the greatness to which we as human beings are summoned. But such an experience says nothing about the acts of which we would be capable at the moment of truth: it says nothing about our *character*. As one might imagine, it is a long way from a vocation for greatness to the carrying out of the great works that alone can provide its confirmation. Kant explains that the sublime is available to us primarily as feeling. But it would be wrong to conclude, on the basis of some sentiment of our possible greatness, that our current sentiments are in fact great, and from there to a general greatness of

9. Kant, *Critique of Judgment*, §28.

10. Ibid. [translation modified].

our character. As long as one is dealing with the aesthetics of the sublime, it is acceptable to talk about a single humanity shared by both he who actually undergoes the perilous experience and he who experiences it aesthetically—that is, he who imagines it. Kant is thus able to say, in describing the spectator of some sublime natural spectacle, that "the humanity in our person is kept from being degraded, even though a human being would have to succumb to that power."[11] Which man is threatened here? Though it is certainly not the spectator, this makes no difference. But if we move from an aesthetic to a practical perspective, the distinction between the actor and the spectator must be reestablished. We can no longer claim that we are all equally great, some of us for standing up to real danger and the rest of us for experiencing noble sentiments. If we are no longer judging the destination of man in general, but rather the force of spirit of particular men, it goes without saying that each of us is endowed with his or her own particular humanity. In short, the sentiment of self constituted by the experience of the sublime is a genuine proof of human grandeur, but only by proxy. In it we recognize the heights of moral nobility to which we are destined to rise. But it would be the height of presumption to draw any conclusions from this about the character that any of us might personally demonstrate in appropriately challenging circumstances, and simply ridiculous to attribute to ourselves the least measure of nobility on the basis of the sublimity of our sentiments.

Consequently it seems to me illegitimate to seek in Kant the recipe for some sort of *politics for intellectuals*, whose defining trait would be their status as pure spectators and whose function, by virtue of this status, would be to *sympathize* from the rear of the hall with whichever side embodies exalted ideas over and against mere empirical interests or affinities. In light of the blunders and hypocrisy associated with the idea of *the committed intellectual*, it seems to me that what ought to appear problematic today is the very notion of a politics for philosophers, one in which political action is limited to the simple appreciation of a Cause without any obligation to take into account either the integrity of its partisans or the appropriateness of the initiatives it undertakes. And whether or not the initiatives are appropriate is some-

---

11. Ibid.

thing that must necessarily be assessed from the perspective of those who will suffer the consequences.

Foucault's 1983 lecture on the Enlightenment includes a commentary on "The Contest of the Faculties" in which he rightly points out that the originality of Kant's view lay in his consideration of the French Revolution as "spectacle" rather than as "gesticulation." Foucault situates the interest of Kant's text for contemporary philosophy precisely in this distinction between gesticulation and spectacle. Though he was well aware that Kant's text suspends political questions in the ordinary sense of the term, Foucault does not thereby conclude that Kant was preoccupied in this text with questions that are more theological (e.g., "Is the world well made?") than political. The key issue for the philosopher is not one of determining "what part of the Revolution should be retained and set up as a model." Foucault surmises that, beyond this question, there is another political decision to be made, one that Kant has invited us to think through. According to Foucault, the question is one of "knowing what is to be made of this will to revolution, this 'enthusiasm' for the Revolution which is something distinct from the revolutionary enterprise itself."[12]

Kant's text would prove particularly valuable for the intellectuals of the 1980s who, though no longer inclined to participate in revolutionary campaigns (i.e., in the Revolution as "gesticulation"), still cling to the prospect of observing the *spectacle* and empathizing with the "good guys." The solution offered by the text would lie in precisely this separation: leave the revolutionary campaigns to the revolutionaries that we are not and have never wholeheartedly been, and let's make something out of our enthusiasm—our desire for some kind of "passionate participation in the Good."[13] The solution is to express our enthusiasm for the spectacle at the same time that we express our reservations about the gesticulation. We have come to the painful realization that revolutions can be disastrous without their having been "betrayed." Dividing the act from its representation allows us to separate the *meaning* of a given uprising from its historical *consequences*. What a "politics for intellec-

12. Michel Foucault, "Kant on Enlightenment and Revolution," trans. Colin Gordon, *Economy and Society* 15:1 (1986): 95 [translation modified].

13. Kant, "The Contest of the Faculties," p. 183 [translation modified].

tuals" would amount to is thus the support of various causes without the necessity of judging their political merits in the ordinary sense of the term. In other words, politics has been eliminated in favor of ethics. Among the professoriat this practice has a long history, but never has it been more clearly formulated than in an article in *Le Monde* where Foucault contrasts the antistrategic ethics of the intellectual with the strategic ethics of those in power. Speaking in the guise of the "strategist," Foucault writes: "What does any one death, any one plaint or any one uprising matter when compared with the overarching necessity of the whole [la grande nécessité de l'ensemble]? On the other hand, what does any one general principle matter to me in the particular situation we now confront?"[14]

By speaking, as he does, of the "overarching necessity of the whole," Foucault leads one to believe that any appeal to action that is based on the requirements of the "whole" is always unwarranted. One will never be justified in expecting the parts to make sacrifices in the name of the whole. Foucault's formula regarding "the overarching necessity of the whole" is suitably vague: it precludes any distinction between totalitarian reasoning and political reasoning, for politics itself, in the ordinary sense of the term, is taken to be the totalitarian threat. *Totalitarian* reasoning invokes the "overarching necessity of the whole" and in its name justifies all manner of massacres and iniquities. This "whole" is by definition a totality that is not only ideal (in that it exists only as representation), but artificial as well: any totality requiring that we pay our tribute of violence and oppression is a totality that can *only* come into being as the result of our mobilization. It is the "humanity of the future" or "the chosen people," for example. Foucault's phrase cannot but call to mind the sophistic slogans of the Stalinist period: that no one is innocent, that everyone's hands are soiled, that history always progresses by violent means, and that a slew of deaths are insignificant when the goal is to give birth to a new humanity. But Foucault's phrase does not exclude the possibility that the totality in

---

14. Michel Foucault, "Is It Useless to Revolt?" trans. James Bernauer, *Philosophy and Social Criticism*, 8:1 (1981): 9 [translation modified]. In this article Foucault responds to those critics who had reproached him for having initially supported Khomeini's "Islamic revolution" in Iran.

question be political, that is, an *existing* totality. *Political* reasoning is that which is carried out from the perspective of a society constituted by the very fact that it must continually confront difficult choices. As an example, one need only consider the difficulties a "strategist" would have in applying Foucault's formula to a situation like that which came out of the Munich accords of 1938. Which "whole," which "we" is to be embraced? Will the self-proclaimed "strategist" be pro- or anti-Munich? Will the "overarching necessity of the whole" serve as a pretext for sacrificing the very people we are supposed to protect (our central European allies), or as a pretext for another massacre of French soldiers (according to the pacifist view)?

As for the "antistrategic" politics of the intellectual, it unfortunately might amount to granting an unlimited exemption from responsibility. "My theoretical ethics is the opposite. It is 'antistrategic': to show respect for acts of revolt on the part of singularities and intransigence whenever power is used in ways contrary to the universal. The choice is simple; carrying it out is often difficult."[15] Thus any act of revolt on the part of a "singularity" is to be respected, regardless of the rights of other "singularities" within the totality in which rights are distributed. Any "universal" that might be set in opposition to such a "singularity" can only be the illusory "overarching necessity of the whole." There is no need to worry about whether some of these "singular" uprisings might not be somewhat disturbing: a singularity (a highly abstract term!) is always right to revolt, not because it needs any reason whatever to do so, but because we know in advance that any universal opposed to it can only be false. Meanwhile, everything is reversed when the intellectual turns his gaze toward those in "power." The authorities who wield power have no right either to assert their own singularity or to plead the particularity of their situation. Only the universal is allotted to them: they are to apply general principles without accommodation. Which amounts to saying that, among those in power, political judgment is out of place.

By means of this master stroke, Foucault manages to unify in one and the same phrase a surrealist ethics calling for a permanent state of exception for the individual, and an ethics more appropriate for horta-

---

15. Ibid., p. 9 [translation modified].

tory and moralistic intellectuals—an unexpected alliance between the
Marquis de Sade and Julien Benda.

The notion of an "intellectual politics" used to have a meaning that
one could discuss and that was worthy of scrutiny, as long as intellectuals could be linked to some highly significant whole. Either intellectuals composed a spiritual authority and belonged to a whole made up
of both a temporal and a spiritual power—the earthly approximation
of the ideal Republic of minds, or alternatively they formed an avant-
garde, in which case they became soldiers in a great army clearing the
way for the worldwide Republic of emancipated workers. Yet Foucault's version of the intellectual does not recognize the validity of *any*
ideal or actual whole. Nor does he envision that one may condemn any
revolt perpetrated by a singularity. In classical terms, a city in which
any singularity is legitimate is a city in thrall to a *tyrant*. A tyrant is
precisely he who exerts power according to the peculiarities [*singu-
larités*] of his own desires rather than in accordance with the "overarching necessity of the whole." In such a city the lie consists in saying
"we," truth in saying "I." Foucault declares that the sole task for
philosophy today is to delineate an "ontology of ourselves." Yet his
mode of thinking leaves no room for "ourselves."

The various "politics of philosophy" that have arisen since Marxism's loss of credibility all partake of what Reinhart Koselleck calls
"critical hypocrisy."[16] What this term refers to is nothing less than a
"figure of spirit" in the Hegelian sense. The "criticism" in question for
Koselleck is the mode of thought proper to the population that, since
the end of the seventeenth century, has inhabited the various societies
of thought forming the Republic of Letters. The way in which these
societies function—as a kind of discussion club where communication
is unimpeded—has come to be taken as the model to be imitated in all
areas of social life. Koselleck demonstrates how this version of the
Republic of Letters develops in the shadow of a total State resting on a
division between politics (reasons of State) and morality (conscience).
Only in the conscience of the king is there a link between political aims
and higher, more universal ones. For their part, the king's subjects,
relieved of all political concerns, are free for the pursuit of pleasure or

16. Reinhart Koselleck, *Critique and Crisis* (Cambridge, Mass: MIT Press, 1988).

the cultivation of the arts. But before too long these deeply apolitical subjects, without looking into the peculiar and fragile conditions that permit them to have free discussions among themselves, come to lay claim to a critical function that legitimately belongs only to whoever incarnates the *universal*. Here what is universal is the point of view of the complete man or that of reason itself. The hypocrisy lies in making political claims grounded in the absence of all politics, or in dissimulating political aims behind a refusal of all political judgment.

In practice, this critical hypocrisy takes the form of an incessant denunciation of superstition and of tyrannical acts. Yesterday's enlightened Philosopher and today's ideological critic both denounce the abuses they observe around them. Yet there can only be *abuses* where there is also *legitimacy* [le bon droit]. An abuse of religion (superstition) is possible only because there also exist legitimate practices of worship. Likewise, power can be abused (tyranny) only if there are also legitimate acts of authority. Critical hypocrisy uncovers abuses everywhere, but fails to provide even the slightest clue as to what a corresponding legitimate practice might be. It is nonetheless clear that if all religious practices are superstitious, there is no need to denounce those that are abusive; one can only privately deplore the frailty of the human spirit. Similarly, if every act of power is arbitrary, there is no reason to protest such power: the best one can do is retreat as far as possible from the territory where such power is wielded.

> The Enlightenment unmasked, reduced, and uncovered, but it failed to see that in the course of this unmasking the essence of the one unmasked becomes dissolved. In the eyes of the hypocritical proponent of Enlightenment, power is identical with the abuse of power. He fails to see that power can act as an inspiration to those who wield it. In the view of the political privateer, power becomes force. Hence in the waning days of the Enlightenment it was held self-evident that a good monarch was worse than an evil one because he prevented the oppressed multitudes from seeing the injustice of the Absolutist principle. The Enlightenment unmasked the king as man, and as man he could be nothing but a usurper.[17]

Born of the division between political affairs, which fall within the jurisdiction of the prince, and moral affairs, whose domain is the

---

17. Ibid., pp. 118–19.

conscience of each individual, the absolutist Enlightenment critic was
not provided with the conceptual framework that would allow him to
come to terms with the political. When he seeks to pass political
judgments, he only manages to make moral pronouncements; and
when, on the other hand, he seeks to make moral pronouncements, he
typically remains oblivious to the political ramifications of his commit-
ments. Even when Enlightenment philosophers contemplate the possibility of a revolution, they do so from an exclusively ethical point of
view. As Koselleck puts it:

> The question is no longer seen in terms of the political contrasting
> of State and civil war but as the moral antithesis of slavery and
> revolution. The general tenor of the Enlightenment is this: revolu-
> tions are necessary. If they do not take place the people are at fault,
> but if they do—and this is the other side of the moral dichotomy—
> then the prince is to blame.[18]

Obviously, the lesson to be drawn from this is *not* that since philosophers and intellectuals know nothing about politics, they have no
business getting mixed up in it. No, the lesson is that it is a mistake to
pass political judgment in such an apolitical way. It is reprehensible
that philosophers should pretend to judge events as if they were seated
in an auditorium rather than onstage like everyone else. Though there
is surely a morality that is universal, there is no such thing as a universal politics. It is simply not possible for philosophers to announce that
everything is political—an outrageous assertion revealing a certain
naiveté—and at the same time refuse to divulge which "whole" they
adhere to and which "overarching necessity" they recognize.

Raymond Aron tells how he came to understand the meaning of the
following important maxim: "Political problems are not moral problems."[19] It happened that in 1932, at a time when he was a young
agrégé[20] full of ideas about the German situation, he made the acquain-
tance of an undersecretary of State: "The minister asked my opinion

---

18. Ibid., p. 161n.

19. Raymond Aron, *Mémoires* (Paris: Julliard, 1983), p. 78.

20. Translator's note: An *agrégé* is one who has been recruited for a teaching position
by the French government after passing a competitive national examination.

and I gave him what I imagine must have been a brilliant speech, in the purest *normalien* style."[21] The undersecretary replied by saying something like, "Your ideas are most illuminating, but what would you do if you were in the shoes of the council president (President Herriot)?" The question is a good one: What would you do if you were in the minister's place? Not that reflection can only be legitimately carried out by putting oneself in the *minister*'s place. But one must put oneself *someplace* within a "whole" and its "overarching necessities"—if not in the minister's place, then in the place of whoever appoints and discharges ministers, or of whoever forms their chief opposition, and so on. The minister asks, "*What would you do in my place?*" The subjects of an absolute monarch never would have imagined that they could have anything to say about such affairs of state. Only later, with the benefit of a long period of civil peace, did such newly *critical* subjects feel it to be within their rights to scrutinize absolutely everything, but *only* in their capacity as thinking beings, *not* as citizens. No more than before did such subjects imagine themselves able to contemplate a given situation from a *political* viewpoint ("in the minister's place," to use a kind of Stendhalian shorthand). For these subjects, this viewpoint is illegitimate: whoever makes any decisions at all is wielding a power that can only have been usurped.

The syndrome of a politics emptied of all political content reappears whenever one seeks to delineate the (always "minimal") program of an intellectual or philosophical politics. This type of program always limits itself to an ethics of conviction or of ultimate ends that is carefully detached from any ethics of responsibility.[22] In practice, it amounts to organizing the shifty movements of one's guilty conscience. Only with a guilty conscience does one obey the king, for one

---

21. Translator's note: A *normalien* is a student at the École Normale Supérieure, one of the most competitive and prestigious of French postsecondary institutions. A "*normalien* style" would thus be that of the French intellectual elite, implying both excessive abstraction and extreme presumption.

22. Max Weber's distinction between these two kinds of ethics is philosophically inadmissible: What sorts of convictions are indifferent to the consequences of the acts they inspire? How can we come to appreciate the responsibilities that fall to each of us if we are without convictions? Nevertheless, this distinction has a certain sociological relevance, to the extent that it isolates a conflict that is ever present in the modern mind.

knows that there should be no king. It is also with a guilty conscience
that one remembers having decapitated the king, for he turned out to
have been a benevolent despot after all, and his "crimes" seem tame
when compared with the patriotic deeds of his successors.

But in the end it should be emphasized that Kant, contrary to the
way he is often portrayed, can in no wise be allied with the idea of a
party of philosopher-spectators. Even if the second section of "The
Contest of the Faculties" is devoted to a question with no immediate
political repercussions, this does not mean that a properly political
point of view is not in some way present in the text. We may be able to
find the elements of a philosophy of political judgment in it, provided
that we direct our attention to the European public considered not as
spectator but as *actor*.

In the first place we should note that, for Kant, it is especially clear
not so much that the European people have the right to adopt a
republican constitution, but that they have the right that every people
has "to give itself a civil constitution of the kind that it sees fit, *without
interference from other powers*."[23] Therefore the first right that should
be mentioned is that which every people has with respect to other
right-bearing subjects, that is, with regard to other peoples. We thus
already know—with a knowledge that is more "reflective" than
"determinative"[24]—who constitutes a people and who does not. We
know whether the French constitute a people. We know whether the
Savoyards are a people distinct from the Franc-Comtois. We know
whether the Piedmontese are a people and whether they form a single
people with the Tuscans. And if we do not know all this, we should
have nothing to say regarding the Cause of the People.

In the second place (and as a student of jurisprudence might remind
us), a right cannot be defined in isolation. The aforementioned right
implies the possibility of intrusion by a foreign people into the government of the people who lay claim to this right. If such a state of
relations between the two powers remains constant, another right held
by the people in question comes to the fore, one that must be recon-

---

23. Kant, "The Contest of the Faculties," p. 182; emphasis mine.

24. Translator's note: This distinction is drawn by Kant in the introduction to the
Critique of Judgment, §IV.

ciled with the first: a people has the right to political institutions assuring its continued existence and security in whatever local circumstances it finds itself. A people has the legitimate expectation that its leaders will have the stature of Heads of State (i.e., that they will look after the "overarching necessities of the whole").

This is why the exertion of political judgment, in the Kantian text that concerns us here, is not to be sought in the body of the text (which is concerned with other kinds of questions), but in notes like this one:

> This does not mean, however, that a people which has a monarchic constitution can thereby claim the right to alter it, or even nurse a secret desire to do so. For a people which occupies extended territories in Europe may feel that monarchy is the only kind of constitution which can enable it to preserve its own existence between powerful neighbors.[25]

Here we approach the threshold where judgment must become political. A given people can demand that its independence be respected. That is, a people can demand this *of its neighbors*, provided that it finds the means to command their respect. But there is no supreme tribunal or universal conscience before which a people can demand that it not be surrounded by powerful neighbors.

What, then, would a philosophy of the *event* of the French Revolution look like? We already know what a study of the *ideas* of the Revolution would amount to: an examination of principles like the rights of man, popular sovereignty, and representative democracy. Since the work would bear mainly on texts, what difference would it make if these texts turned out to be pure speculation—that is, if the Revolution had never taken place? A Revolution reduced to a set of ideas, a Revolution *in principle*, is what the philosophistic conception of the event amounts to. The fact that the Revolution takes place means that ideas become motives for actions and pretexts for revolutionary decisions and judgments. As a result, it is tempting to exchange this noisy business for a more civilized topic of study: the Enlightenment. But even this topic may seem too varied and cacophonous: there is the English Enlightenment, the Scottish Enlightenment, the French

---

25. Kant, "The Contest of the Faculties," p. 182n.

Lumières, the *Aufklärung*. It did not take long for French authors to start using the German term themselves, a term that has the advantage of being better defined, better articulated, and thus better protected from historical vicissitudes. The word *Aufklärung* has the virtue of saving us work by providing its own definition. The *Aufklärung* is no more nor less than what Kant says it is in his famous text, *Was ist Aufklärung?* Once we have settled on this term, there is nothing to stop us from practicing the philosophy of modernity as a sort of "explication de texte."

It is true that each of the exchanges of an unwieldy object of study for a calmer portion of the same object is not without justification. The transformation of Europe in the eighteenth century was above all a change in representations and ideals. Moreover, one may claim that the *Aufklärung* should be privileged: the *Aufklärer*, because of their proximity to the traditional world, went further than either the Enlightenment or the *Lumières* in explicitly and rationally delineating the new principles. Finally, Kant's text is manifestly important and must be taken into account by any serious attempt to come to terms with the epoch.

Be that as it may, throughout these different exchanges the object of study has been continually purified. Having begun with a historical explosion of European proportions, we have ended up writing expositions on Kantian philosophy. Now of course it is perfectly natural that an author writing in German and discussing the subject from the perspective of German history should use the word *Aufklärung*. What I mean by this is not only that *Aufklärung* is the German word, but that the actual thing that the word *Aufklärung* refers to is part of Kant's heritage: namely, the *Lumières* minus a revolution in one's own country. By contrast, one has to wonder what motivates those authors writing in French who choose to use the German word rather than the French one, when there is no historical justification for making the French *Lumières* depend on the German *Aufklärung*. If in recurring to the German word they mean to indicate that the Enlightenment is, historically, a European phenomenon, why not use the English word "Enlightenment"? It is difficult to avoid the suspicion that what is at work here is a desire to *sanitize* the epoch, to view it only in the best light. There is always something superficial about an ascent that moves too quickly from the flux of *time* to the lofty heights of the *concept*.

A philosophy of the French Revolution should take care to avoid such philosophistic procedures. Such a philosophy would not be reduced to simply narrating yet again the course of past events, nor would it merely mirror the down-to-earth historical narrative with an account of more spiritually exalting events. The philosophy of the French Revolution will provide reasons, if indeed there are any, to prefer one version of the historical event over another. Why are certain reconstructions of the event preferable to others? The question is partly a factual one, to be decided by digging through archives, and partly a philosophical one, because one must gauge the relative importance of the various "factors" involved: the ideas, institutions, and interests, among other things. Indeed, the very definition of what constitutes a factor—politics, religion, etcetera—implies an entire philosophy.

In short, the role of a philosophy of historical events is not to present another—philosophical—report on the course of those events. Rather, it is to help us to understand and judge what is reported in the press (and repeated by the public), and it can do this only by improving the conceptual apparatus through which we attempt to understand, in any given situation, what is going on in the world.

=3=

Modern Beauty

There is no lack of subjects, nor of colours, to make epics. The painter, the true painter . . . will be he who can snatch its epic quality from the life of today and can make us see and understand, with brush or with pencil, how great and poetic we are in our cravats and our patent-leather boots.

Baudelaire, "The Salon of 1845"[1]

In recent years, Jürgen Habermas has again raised the question concerning a "philosophical discourse of modernity."[2] As Habermas describes it in his book of the same name, this question bears not so much on what the Moderns have had to say in philosophy, as on what they have had to say about themselves. And Habermas never doubts for an instant that the most important things the Moderns have had to say about themselves are to be found in philosophical works.

Habermas's book begins with a citation of Max Weber. Throughout his own work, Weber asked this question: Why has the process of *rationalization*—which is for Weber the defining trait of the modern age—occurred only in the West and not, for example, in China? By "process of rationalization" Weber referred to the process by which the image of the world becomes disenchanted, the process of *Entzauberung*. But five pages after his reference to Weber, Habermas substitutes for it a reference to Hegel, inviting us to recognize the reason discussed by philosophers in what the sociologist calls "rationalization." Habermas explains this shift in the following way: "He-

---

1. Charles Baudelaire, "The Salon of 1845," in *The Mirror of Art*, ed. and trans. Jonathan Mayne (London: Phaidon, 1955), p. 38.

2. Jürgen Habermas, *The Philosophical Discourse of Modernity*, trans. Frederick Lawrence (Cambridge, Mass.: MIT Press, 1987).

gel was the first philosopher to develop a clear concept of modernity. We have to go back to him if we want to understand the internal relationship between modernity and rationality, which, until Max Weber, remained self-evident and which today is being called into question."[3] It never occurs to Habermas that the sociologist might be in a better position than the philosopher to assess what is truly modern.

Habermas explains that in Max Weber's day it went without saying that the more modern things were, the more they were subject to rational norms. Today this presumed rational validity of the "modern project" has been put in question, not in virtue of any shortcomings in its execution, but with regard to its very concept.[4] The heirs of the modern project had grown used to being attacked from the right by partisans of the old, counter-revolutionary, antimodern school. Today they find themselves overwhelmed from the left by a new critical movement that also has it in for modern ideals, a kind of ultraleft made up mostly of French disciples of Nietzsche and Heidegger. Habermas takes it upon himself to show that these more recent critics are less radical, less *advanced*, than they imagine. In his view, the "postmodern" is nothing more than the reincarnation of the "antimodern" perspective, presenting itself as a *Nachaufklärung* while perpetuating the tradition of the *Gegenaufklärung*.[5]

Habermas reduces the Hegelian indices of what is modern to four points:[6]

1. moral *individualism*
2. the *right to criticism*, or the freedom of conscience
3. the *autonomy of action* (who I am depends on what I do and not on who my ancestors were)
4. *idealistic philosophy*

---

3. Ibid., p. 4.

4. See Habermas's article "Modernity: An Incomplete Project," trans. Seyla Ben-Habib, in *The Anti-Aesthetic: Essays on Postmodern Culture*, ed. Hal Foster (Port Townsend, Wash.: Bay Press, 1983), pp. 3–15.

5. Habermas, *The Philosophical Discourse of Modernity*, p. 5.

6. Ibid., p. 17.

It is this last point that is most obviously problematic. For one might argue that the truly modern philosophy is *empiricism*, the rejection of all extraneous authority. Or, by another view, that it is *positivism*, the decision to separate facts from our attitudes toward them. Or it might be *pragmatism*, the idea that, contrary to what ancient philosophers believed, it is not necessary to provide an ultimate foundation or ground for our judgments. Or finally, one might make a claim, as Max Weber himself no doubt would, for *existentialism*: the modern "discovery" that all our truths and principles depend on a personal, radical, and consequently unjustifiable choice.

If one asked a classically educated French reader to name the first thinker to conceive the historical principle of the modern age, he would no doubt designate Condorcet (and then, in turn, his disciple Auguste Comte). The French were slow to give Hegel his due. It was only through the teachings of Kojève and the German immigrants of the 1930s that the French came to the view that Hegel was the philosopher who raised the modern epoch to the level of the concept. Simply put, the fact that Hegel's "dialectical reason" had come to replace the "analytical reason" of Condorcet could mean only one thing: that the society engendered by the Russian Revolution was more advanced than those governed according to the principles of liberal democracy (which, in the mind of the French public, were the direct result of the French Revolution).

Habermas is clearly unaware that by "Hegelianizing" so decisively he is privileging a particular national tradition. A sociologist would have less difficulty recognizing that the philosophical consciousness of the modern situation has been differently expressed within various national cultures. Habermas apparently fails to see that without a historical agent his "modern project" can only be chimerical. Indeed, the Idea's empirical support is neither the human race nor an individual thinker, but the system formed by *distinct* societies whose interactions make up what appears to us as a single process taking place on the scale of the West as a whole. The philosopher does not hesitate to describe a modern project of rationalization in the singular. But from the perspective of a sociological analysis, the dynamic that for us is constitutive of the worldwide process of modernization is itself the

result of a complex play of exchanges between societies that are cultur-
ally distinct.[7]

But the French reader's difficulties start with the very title of
Habermas's book in German: *Der philosophische Diskurs der Moderne*. To translate the German *die Moderne* into French, the word
modernité is correct, for philologists tell us that the German word
came into fashion at the end of the nineteenth century precisely in
order to refer to modernity in Baudelaire's sense of the term.[8] In
Baudelaire's wake we have come to understand modernity as a kind of
inspiration opposed to the academicism perpetuating the classical canon. This is why Baudelaire asked: "Who will be the painter of modern
life?" Habermas, by contrast, asks who will be its *thinker*. And he
answers: Hegel. For us, this answer is preposterous. Though it is conceivable that Hegel's philosophy of history expressed the principle of
the modern age [*die Neuzeit*], it is impossible to see his philosophy as
the anticipation of a modernity that Baudelaire will later seek in Stendhal, Balzac and, more generally, in the "peinture des moeurs" of the
July Monarchy and the Second Empire.

To put this conceptual point in the terms of logical grammar, we
might say that Habermas turns the substantive "modernity" into the
designation of a distinctive property. For him, modernity is what
makes the modern—a modern mind, a modern work, or modern
times—*modern*. In other words, modernity is the characteristic that
allows us to assign things to the modern age rather than to another.
This means that the noun "modernity" is to the adjective "modern" as
the substantive "humidity" is to the adjective "humid," or the word
"elasticity" to the adjective "elastic." For Habermas, *modernity is a
property*. That is why he is able to bring together under the banner of
Modernity all the various stages that constitute, according to the most
widely accepted chronology, the modern age:

---

7. See Louis Dumont, "Identités collectives et idéologie universaliste: leur interaction
de fait," *Critique*, no. 456 (1985), pp. 506–18.

8. See Hans Robert Jauss's study, "Literarische Tradition und gegenwärtiges Be-
wußtsein der Modernität," in *Literaturgeschichte als Provokation* (Frankfurt: Suhrkamp, 1970), pp. 11–12.

1. the manifestations of a new way of thinking in the sciences, in the
   arts, in law, and in politics (these manifestations, in the Renaissance
   and the seventeenth century, mark the beginning of the modern age);
2. the ideas and aspirations of the enlightened minds of the eighteenth
   century, which, taken as a whole, make up what Habermas aptly
   refers to as the "modern project" (the century of the Enlightenment
   or *Aufklärung*);
3. contemporary philosophies of the French Revolution, that is, of the
   event that was widely considered at the time as a putting to the test
   of the modern project (German idealism);
4. and finally, "modernity" in Baudelaire's sense, which Habermas is
   too quick to place in the aesthetic sphere.

Unfortunately Habermas, who follows Walter Benjamin in his reading of Baudelaire, does not take Baudelaire's conception of modernity
seriously enough.[9] It would be a mistake to see this as a minor detail.
Any conception of the whole of modernity must provide a place not
only for the poet's images, but also for the critic's ideas. Habermas
feels no need to move beyond an *aesthetic* reading of Baudelaire: he
thinks that one can come to a philosophical understanding of Baudelaire through Kant. In my opinion this is why Baudelaire's conception
of modernity completely escapes him and, along with it, an important
part of modernity *tout court*.

An artistic modernity that limited its claims to the aesthetic realm
would be a version of romanticism, as the word is commonly understood. Indeed, Habermas distinguishes as many spheres of human
activity, governed by the instituted rules of a culture, as there are types
of rational legislation in Kant's critical philosophy. This reduction *in
principle* of all culture to philosophy provides a truly glaring example
of philosophism. We know that, for Kant, there are three domains in
which reason legislates. First, there is the rational legislation over the
construction of valid explanations of natural phenomena. For exam-

---

9. Benjamin in this case shared the opinion of André Gide: "To judge Baudelaire's
intellectual power by his philosophical excurses would be a major error": Walter Benjamin, "Central Park," trans. Lloyd Spencer and Mark Harrington, *New German Critique*, no. 34 (1985), p. 41. For a countervailing view, one might consult Pierre Pachet's
book *Le premier venu: essai sur la politique de Baudelaire* (Paris: Denoël, 1976).

ple, according to Kant, we know in advance (and this knowledge is rational) that such phenomena are neither miraculous nor fortuitous. There is a second rational legislation over our practical decisions, by which we must neither treat people like things nor things like people. Finally, there is a third rational legislation over the expression of our aesthetic judgments, one guaranteeing that it will be possible to communicate an authentically aesthetic pleasure to others, even though such pleasure is subjective. This organization of "modern rationality" is taken to be the organization of rationality *as such* by those who think they have a "transcendental argument" proving its necessity. Such an argument purports to show how any reasonable being *must* (logically) recognize the autonomy of the three spheres and the legislation proper to each.

From within modern rationality, it is legitimate to exalt the autonomy of the aesthetic viewpoint as long as the claim does not exceed the limits of the aesthetic sphere. On the other hand, it is illegitimate to attempt to subordinate ethics and science to aesthetics. From this rationalist perspective, *romanticism* represents the discovery and enthusiastic affirmation of the aesthetic autonomy of the subject: the artistic genius is exempt from the rules; eccentric subjectivity is beyond mere convention. This is where modernity in Baudelaire's sense will come to be interpreted as *merely* aesthetic by those rationalists who know only one sort of romanticism. Indeed, in the context of European romanticism, these rationalists often cite Baudelaire as having accentuated the possibilities for aesthetic provocation: the instant, the fleeting, the stimulating, the *bizarre*.[10]

Moreover, Habermas insists, it is in the aesthetic domain that an awareness of *being modern* first arose among the Moderns. In the "querelle des Anciens et des Modernes" Habermas finds the means of introducing his philosophical conception of modern reason as a reason grounded on itself. He writes:

> The problem of grounding modernity out of itself first comes to consciousness in the realm of aesthetic criticism. This becomes clear when one traces the history of the concept "modern." The process

---

10. Habermas summarizes this reading of Baudelaire—the most common one—in *The Philosophical Discourse of Modernity*, pp. 8–11.

of detachment from the models of ancient art was set going in the early eighteenth century by the famous *querelle des Anciens et des Modernes*. The party of the moderns rebelled against the self-understanding of French classicism by assimilating the aesthetic concept of perfection to that of progress as it was suggested by modern natural science.[11]

What is properly modern, according to Habermas, is to seek to develop models and rules for success on one's own, rather than passively receiving them from some traditional authority. By this interpretation, the position of the Ancients embodies a heteronomous reason, whereas the Modern position is the expression of the new ("modern") stance of autonomous reason.

It is also in the aesthetic realm that the antimodern *avant-garde* arises, effectively transforming romanticism into the nihilism that Habermas deplores. German romanticism had already anticipated the return of Dionysus. But even so, it upheld the unity of poetry and philosophy, the lofty marriage of exalted myth and liberating reason. Nihilism disrupts this unity by calling for the return of Dionysus, but in order to liberate us from Socrates and his tyranny of reason.

In this context Habermas comes to cite the remarkable text known as "The Earliest System-Programme of German Idealism," which dates from 1796. This text, in Hegel's handwriting, was apparently composed by Schelling, under Hölderlin's influence. As Habermas points out, the text maintains the unity of reason because it reconciles the three transcendental properties: Goodness and Truth are united in Beauty. "I am now convinced that the highest act of Reason, the one through which it encompasses all Ideas, is an aesthetic act, and that *truth and goodness only become sisters in beauty*—the philosopher must possess just as much aesthetic power as the poet."[12] The text concludes that aesthetic philosophy must be presented in the form of a "mythology of reason" in order to make possible the complete equality of all the individuals in a free community.

---

11. Ibid., p. 8.

12. "The 'Earliest System-Programme of German Idealism,' " in H. S. Harris, *Hegel's Development: Toward the Sunlight, 1770–1801* (Oxford: Clarendon Press, 1972), p. 511.

> We must have a new mythology, but this mythology must be in the service of Ideas; it must be a mythology of *Reason*.
>
> Until we express the Ideas aesthetically, i.e., mythologically, they have no interest for the *people*, and conversely until mythology is rational the philosopher must be ashamed of it. Thus in the end enlightened and unenlightened must clasp hands, mythology must become philosophical in order to make the people rational, and philosophy must become mythological in order to make the philosophers sensible. . . . Then reigns eternal unity among us.[13]

In this text, myth is not the voice of some original Foundation or Other of reason. Rather, it is a translation of philosophy into images the people can understand. Here the rational unity of beauty, goodness, and truth has thus not yet been repudiated.

Yet perhaps the entire problem posed by a philosophy of "modernity" amounts to this: is the *modern notion of beauty* one that is separated from goodness and truth, or is it somehow rationally tied to them? According to Habermas, the error made by Nietzsche and his heirs was to push the autonomy of the beautiful to the point of separation. For Nietzsche, taste is the organ of a superior knowledge, one that is beyond good and evil just as it is beyond truth and error in the usual sense of these words. Of course the autonomy of aesthetic experience is a typically modern idea. In Habermas's view, Nietzsche is unaware he has projected into an archaic past an experience that is only possible *today*.[14]

But here Habermas is missing the important point: modernity in its Baudelairean incarnation is completely unconcerned with "l'école païenne." It wants nothing to do with the Greeks and Romans—"and the seething Achilles, and the prudent Ulysses, and the wise Penelope, and Telemachus the overgrown clod, and the beautiful Helen who lost Troy, and the burning Sappho, the patroness of all hysterics."[15] Baudelairean modernity is devoid of the nostalgia for Dionysus or the anticipation of the "God-to-come." Unconcerned by the "lack of divine

---

13. Ibid., pp. 511–12.

14. Habermas, *The Philosophical Discourse of Modernity*, p. 96.

15. Charles Baudelaire, "L'école païenne," in *Oeuvres complètes*, ed. Marcel A. Ruff (Paris: Seuil, 1968), p. 300.

names," it is secure in the knowledge that there is no shortage of myths and legends, that we have our own particular beauty and heroism. In this regard, it is also uncertain whether Nietzsche can be construed as an entirely romantic writer. For one finds in Nietzsche a broad critique of romanticism as stemming from a feebleness of both head *and* heart. In fact, Nietzschean inspiration is not incompatible with the modern, *Parisian* gaiety of an Offenbach, as a reading of the books of Clément Rosset will attest.[16]

What should by now be seen as highly questionable is the excessively literary conception of myth as mere marvelous stories or the *gift of a poem* that the poet bestows on his people. In an insightful article on "Myth in the Eighteenth Century,"[17] Jean Starobinski has described the literary past that prepared the aspirations of romanticism for an anthropogenetic Myth. Starobinski's demonstration requires that we reject Habermas's version of the "querelle des Anciens et des Modernes."

In order to assess the status of ancient myths in the age of classicism, one must make a distinction between fable and mythology. *Fable* comprises the set of notions about pagan divinities that form the "artistic heritage." This communal treasury of stories, images, and motifs is utilized by all the arts. By contrast, *mythology* is a body of knowledge developed by scholars that combines historical research on the (usually literary) sources of ancient theological fables on the one hand, and hypotheses on the origins of those fables on the other. What is the position of *fable* within French classical culture? It occupies the profane pole, whereas the *one true religion* defines the sacred pole. The crucial point is that, in the seventeenth century, one spoke of "fable" and not of "myth" as we do. The word "fable" immediately betrays the fictitious nature of what it designates, thereby allowing classical

---

16. See Clément Rosset, *L'anti-nature* (Paris: Presses Universitaires de France, 1973), pp. 120–23. According to Rosset, Offenbach's gaiety is remarkable for expressing the idea that life must be affirmed not because it is beautiful but because it remains life even when it is false. In fragments dating from 1887–88, Nietzsche praises Offenbach's free spirit, juxtaposing Offenbach's musical vivacity with what he sees as the ponderousness of Wagner.

17. Jean Starobinski, "Le mythe au XVIIIᵉ siècle," *Critique*, no. 366 (1977), pp. 975–97.

French culture to practice a false religion alongside the true, but only on the condition that the false one not be believed in. Such a cultural arrangement is hierarchical: there is of course only one true religion—biblical monotheism—but Counterreformation Christianity also allots an inferior place to the universe of polytheistic drives. "Through its avowed lack of truth value, fable is a clear indication of the futility of human existence."[18] In fable, the sinful desires for pleasure, power, or glory are not denied. Rather, they are acknowledged and rendered trivial by their openly fictitious representation. At its height, French classical culture is marked by the duality of the festival:

> Mythological fiction makes possible a kind of praiseful hyperbole that could never have been uttered within the constraints of Christian traditions. After a victory in battle, the Christian festival culminates in the worship of the God of armies: *Te Deum laudamus.* . . . But the Christian festival is doubled by a profane and *mythological* festival which exalts the prince himself by comparing him to Mars or Hercules. . . . This "make-believe" divinization gives rise to heights of celebratory energy which, though confined within the Greco-Roman model, permit all manner of excesses precisely because such excesses never purport to be anything other than simulacra. The Sun-King may dance in the costume of Apollo, and Jupiter descend from the heavens in a stage prop in order to announce an illustrious royal lineage to the centuries to come.[19]

It seems to me that there is an echo of this fictive worship that always verges on worshiping fictions in Baudelaire's aphorism: "To glorify the worship of images (my great, my unique, my primitive passion)."[20] An astonishing notion—glorifying worship—when all worship itself attests to the glory of that which is worthy. Here the worship of images is authorized, on the condition that it be understood its object is the divinity of images that have no truth value, and not a divinity that the holy image would derive from being the true image of a divine being. Certainly, from the more severe perspective of a strictly biblical religion, baroque art can only be idolatrous. However, it is also to be noted that,

18. Ibid., p. 980.

19. Ibid., p. 983.

20. Baudelaire, "Mon coeur mis à nu" (no. 38), in *Oeuvres complètes,* p. 638.

in Catholic countries, the solution provided by the doubling of worship is reproduced within sacred art itself, often resulting in sensuous, and even astonishingly sensual, representations of the divine. Conversely, puritanical spirituality often gives rise to iconoclasm.

What is remarkable is that the invitation to choose a subject from ancient fables is not felt as a constraint by the artist—not initially, at least—but rather as a support, a license for the "imaginary satisfaction" of desire. And this license is granted only on the condition that desire find its satisfaction in the forms of classical mythology, and not in some original expression produced by the artist himself.

But all this amounts to saying that French classical culture invented the autonomy of art: a distinction, never before drawn on such a scale, between the sacred realm subject to the authority of the Church as the guardian of Truth, and the profane realm, where one may derive pleasure from simulacra. In short, French classical culture is at the origin of the thoroughly modern conception of art as a free play of the imagination, as that domain of human existence dedicated to glittering appearance, to the gleam of fiction, and to the various disguises that make desire palatable. And if this is the case, Habermas's assessment of the "querelle des Anciens et des Modernes" will have to be inverted. Indeed, the more *modernist* of the two factions is not, as Habermas believes, the faction advocating progress, but rather that of the partisans of the canonization of classical forms. Recall that the *querelle* began as a dispute about the relative merits of the "merveilleux chrétien" and the "merveilleux païen."[21] The partisans of the Modern want our art to be as truthful as our religion. They do not believe in classical perfection and thus continue the tradition of innovation that, from the Carolingian to the Italian Renaissance, was characteristic of Western art. What is new in this is that the last of these inventions presents itself as a *renaissance*, as a return to a model of perfection that had been forgotten during the "Middle Ages." As for the party of the Ancients, it can neither be traditional nor promote the tradition, for there is at that time, quite simply, no tradition of classicism. The

---

21. Translator's note: *Merveilleux* is the word used in classical French to translate Aristotle's *thaumaston*, a word usually translated into English as "the marvelous" or "the wonderful." See *Poetics*, 1460ª12.

imitation of the ancients is a new principle. The invention of a canon instituted something called "art," an art liberated from religion but only on the condition that it accept the subordinate status accorded to entertainment and ornamentation. The doctrine of the imitation of the ancients allowed art to detach itself from any concern for ultimate truths, just as the State at that time had detached itself from concern for the sovereign good.

This classical balance between sacred and profane came undone fairly quickly. As early as the mid-eighteenth century, the turn to ancient fable had lapsed into academicism. There arose a general feeling that mythical poetry had become too frivolous and was in need of sacred inspiration. On the other hand, critical histories of mythology came to view fable as the result of an imagination spurred by primitive passions. They suggested that ancient myths are productions of the human mind, a kind of poetry that early men must have believed out of their excessive gullibility. This complicity between poetry and fable laid out in advance the road later taken by the poetic revolution of the romantics, whose defense of poetry was inextricably tied to a rehabilitation of myth. This explains their mistaken expectation that the poets would set in place a new mythology. Indeed, the same minds who had rebelled against the conventionality of fable nevertheless still conceived this future myth according to the models provided by classical fable. This new myth is still characterized as a kind of great poem in which the age will come to recognize the palpable truth it was waiting for. Starobinski concludes his essay as follows:

> Myth, which at the beginning of the eighteenth century had been purely *profane* ornament, became preeminently *sacred*—that is, something that imposes its law in advance and, in the last instance, determines human values—in its capacity as ultimate authority. . . . This change is the corollary of another one: what had been *sacred* at the beginning of the eighteenth century—scriptural revelation, tradition, dogma—was now subject to a "demystifying" critique. It was thus reduced to being nothing more than a human production, a mythical fabrication. . . . The great Myth which was anticipated at that time—and which never came to be—was no longer a theogony, but an anthropogony. Such a Myth would have assembled the people by proclaiming the advent of the Man-God who produces himself through this very proclamation, or through the work of his

hands. All the mythologies of the modern world are but the pale substitutes of this great, incomplete Myth.[22]

So what does this have to do with *modern beauty*?

It is not difficult to extract from Baudelaire's criticism a number of declarations in favor of art for art's sake. These texts support the idea that "modern reason" seeks to separate from one another our various reasons for approving or condemning something. Thus something might be beautiful yet false or bad. Moreover, Baudelaire explicitly upholds the Kantian tripartite division of judgments, taking it up while attributing it to Edgar Allan Poe.

But how is it that one finds declarations from Baudelaire of that purport in a text that is violently hostile to what presents itself as modern?

> Bizarre heresies have found their way into literary criticism. Some impenetrable cloud from Geneva, Boston or Hell, has blotted out the beautiful rays of the sun of aesthetics. The infamous doctrine of the inseparability of the Beautiful, the True, and the Good is an invention of modern philosophication [la philosophaillerie moderne] (by what strange contagion are we led to use the jargon of madness in our attempt to define it!).[23]

The same Baudelairean texts on Edgar Allan Poe that denounce the "heresy of didacticism" attribute this error to the "philosophy of progress," that is, to the ideas of the Enlightenment. In these texts Baudelaire sarcastically rails against democracy (for forbidding "the expansion of individualities"), against "blasphemous love and liberty," against the "century infatuated with itself," against "Americanism" and "Americomania." He explicitly associates the worship of the beautiful with the civilization of the ancien régime. If the American social milieu is unfavorable for poetry, he claims, it is because America lacks a State, a capital that would be "its brain and its sun," in short, an aristocracy.[24] On the other hand, whenever Baudelaire wants to ma-

---

22. Starobinski, "Le mythe au XVIIIᵉ siècle," p. 997.

23. Baudelaire, "Théophile Gautier," in *Selected Writings on Art and Artists*, trans. P. E. Charvet (Cambridge: Cambridge University Press, 1972), p. 265 [translation modified].

24. Baudelaire, "Further Notes on Edgar Poe," in *Selected Writings on Art and Artists*, p. 197 [translation modified].

lign the "puerile utopia of *art for art's sake*,"[25] he is perfectly happy to invert the above-mentioned views. For example, in his attack on the "école païenne," he condemns the "immoderate taste for form,"[26] whereas in "Further Notes on Edgar Poe" he praises the American poet's "immoderate taste for beautiful forms."[27]

It is worth noting that none of the preceding texts suggests that there might be such a thing as a history of taste. Evidently, the situation is altogether different for the texts concerned with modernity. There Baudelaire makes no attempt to hide his agreement with Stendhal:

> For me, Romanticism is the most recent, the most up-to-date expression of the beautiful.
> There are as many forms of beauty as there are habitual ways of seeking happiness.
> The philosophy of progress explains this clearly; thus, just as there have been as many ideals as there have been, for all peoples, ways of understanding morality, love, religion, etc., so romanticism consists, not in technical perfection, but in a conception analogous to the morality of the age.[28]

This idea of a beauty that is relative to time came to Baudelaire from the "philosophy of progress," that is, from the protosociological line of thought that runs from Montesquieu to Stendhal's mentors from the school of the Idéologues. Just as there is no one political regime ideal for all people, so there is no one definition of beauty. Each time one must take into account climate and temperament, education and customs. In the absence of this kind of sociological description of a people, its taste remains unintelligible. Thus the relativity of the beautiful over time that is implied by the notion of a specifically *modern* beauty, should not be understood as a kind of commonplace regarding the charm of past eras never to be seen again. The time in question here is the *century*, the *epoch*, and refers to certain specific customs and passions. Baudelaire cites Stendhal: "Painting is nothing but con-

---

25. Baudelaire, "Pierre Dupont," in *Oeuvres complètes,* p. 291.

26. Baudelaire, "L'école païenne," p. 301.

27. Baudelaire, "Further Notes on Edgar Poe," p. 206 [translation modified].

28. Baudelaire, "The Salon of 1846," in *Selected Writings on Art and Artists*, pp. 52–53 [translation modified].

structed morality."[29] This morality has nothing to do with an ethics of rational obligations, as a Kantian would understand it. Rather, it is the manner in which happiness is pursued at a given time.

And here a transcendental definition of the beautiful as "exact proportion"[30] is no longer sufficient. Beauty is granted a larger sphere, in that forms are taken as referring to a moral ideal of grandeur. Modern life has its own particular beauty because it also has its own sense of grandeur, its own heroism, which amounts to saying that romanticism, as Baudelaire speaks of it here, is understood in the active and energetic sense given to it by Stendhal and not in the sense of German romanticism.

In his *Histoire de la peinture en Italie,* Stendhal explains that the "ancient ideal of beauty" is above all to be sought in ancient statuary as the idealization of martial and civic force. The ancient hero is an athlete. But what would an athlete look like in a modern-day salon? "It seems to me that you would not want Milo of Croton as one of your friends."[31] Ancient grace is what force becomes when it is contained, mastered, and educated toward civic ends. The ancient ideal of beauty has nothing to do with *charm, slenderness, vivacity, gaiety, spirit,* or *refinement,* qualities that we Moderns see as the essential ingredients of beauty. Where the ancients looked for a display of reserved force, we expect *elegance.* And this is simply because physical force is no longer as desirable in an age where war is waged with firearms.

Stendhal advances the following principle:

> Modern beauty is founded on the general lack of resemblance that separates life in the salon from life in the forum. . . .
> Leonidas, who had such stature when he wrote the inscription "Passerby, go tell Sparta . . . , etc.," might have been—indeed, most definitely was—a most insipid lover, friend, and husband.[32]

---

29. Stendhal, *Histoire de la peinture en Italie*, ed. Paul Arbelet, new edition ed. Victor Del Litto and Ernest Abranavel (Geneva: Slatkine Reprints, 1986), II, 226.

30. Baudelaire, "Edgar Allan Poe: His Life and Works," in *Selected Writings on Art and Artists*, p. 166.

31. Stendhal, *Histoire de la peinture en Italie*, p. 116.

32. Ibid., p. 138.

Stendhal is clear on this point: modern manners are gentle. A modern man is someone who feels that there should be no war. Stendhal felt that total war was a thing of the past. In Greece, if wars were not won, the city was destroyed, the men slaughtered, and the women led into captivity. Stendhal's "philosophy of progress" forces him to view the Napoleonic wars as a relapse into ancient customs. Napoleon's mistake was to have disturbed the slumber of the "good Germans": "They ended up rebelling and, guided by the lance of the Cossack, they came and gave us a sample of ancient wars."[33] By this Stendhal means to suggest that in a normal age people never have a chance to see a war or wear a uniform. Stendhal is too much a disciple of the Philosophes to come to terms with the meaning of his own wanderings across Europe under Napoleon. Just as he was incapable of understanding how the Spanish peasants were able to take up arms to defend their churches and their reactionary principles, so Stendhal was unable to foresee the warlike and nationalistic features of the new century.

Baudelaire retained the opposition between the *forum* and the *salon*. What he at first called "romanticism" and later "modernity" is above all a spirit of emancipation with regard to the various dogmas of artistic Jacobinism. The "imperial, republican school" had put into practice a return to the ancients, subordinating painting to sculpture. Though he extols Delacroix ("the leader of the *modern* school")[34] for having liberated painting, Baudelaire is still quite far from any "formalistic" conception of pictorial beauty. In his eulogy of Delacroix, he praises the use of both drawing and color. Through *contour* Delacroix expresses "man's gesture, however violent"; through *color* he renders the "atmosphere of the human drama."[35] In the same text Baudelaire reminds us that Delacroix's father belonged to that "race of strong men" who were at first revolutionaries and later became Bonapartists. In order to describe Delacroix's power, Baudelaire recurs to a language one would naturally use to describe Napoleon's military art. Of the style of Delacroix, he writes that it is marked by "concision and a kind

33. Ibid., p. 134.

34. Baudelaire, "The Salon of 1846," p. 59.

35. Baudelaire, "The Life and Work of Eugène Delacroix," in *Selected Writings on Art and Artists*, p. 361.

of intensity without ostentation, the usual result of concentrating the whole of one's mental powers on a given point."[36]

In short, Baudelaire's conception of the beautiful can in no wise be seen as aesthetic, for it upsets the entire tripartite arrangement of "modern rationality." For Baudelaire, it is not aesthetics but poetics, taken in an Aristotelian sense as the theory of human drama, that determines the proper use of the word "beautiful." This is why it is not immaterial that the characterization of modernity was first formulated in art criticism and not as part of some philosophy of history. Indeed, art criticism, as Baudelaire practices it, is moral criticism. The painter who depicts the mores and customs of modern life is a painter of modern mores. The critic's task then becomes that proposed by Stendhal: to be attentive to modernity is to follow the modifications that *force* undergoes. What becomes of human force when the social milieu changes? Baudelaire was intensely interested in the phenomenon of dandyism precisely because it is one form taken by the search for grandeur. In Baudelaire's conception, a *dandy* is an "unemployed Hercules"[37] or, as Stendhal might have it, a modern hero. Indeed, Baudelaire had planned to write an essay on "dandyism in literature" under the title: "Literary Dandyism, or Grandeur Without Convictions."[38]

When Baudelaire writes about modernity, he thinks sociologically. Just like Habermas, Baudelaire says that every epoch is moved by a "philosophical thinking." And how are we to uncover this thinking? Not by looking among philosophers for "reason founded on itself," but by comparing the engravings in which fashions are depicted:

> If an impartially minded man were to look through the *whole* range of French fashions, from the origins of France to the present day, he would find nothing to shock or even to surprise him. The transitions would be as elaborately articulated as they are in the ranks of the

---

36. Ibid., p. 372 [translation modified]. One should keep in mind the meaning Baudelaire gives to his evocations of Napoleon: "Napoleon is a substantive that means 'domination' " ("L'esprit et le style de Villemain," in *Oeuvres complètes*, p. 501).

37. Baudelaire, "The Painter of Modern Life," in *Selected Writings on Art and Artists*, p. 422.

38. Charles Baudelaire, Letter to Auguste Poulet-Malassis, 4 February 1860, in *Correspondance*, ed. Claude Pichois and Jean Ziegler (Paris: Gallimard, 1973), I, 664.

animal kingdom. . . . And if to the illustration representing each age he were to add the philosophic thought with which that age was most preoccupied or concerned—the thought being inevitably called to mind by the illustration—he would see what a deep harmony governs all the branches of history.[39]

Fashions that might seem shocking or ridiculous to us, if we were to judge them from some *academic* or absolutist perspective, seem charming, if we can trace the *transitions*. An academic eye sees barbaric forms in everything but its own abstractions, precisely because it is indifferent to the transitions between such forms and unconcerned with learning the reasons behind local customs. By contrast, the painter of modern life is a "man of the world": "By 'man of the world,' I mean a man of the whole world, a man who understands the world and the mysterious and legitimate reasons for all its customs."[40] One might well suppose that Baudelaire would have seen Habermas's *modern project* as a program for a kind of generalized academicism. For critical theory still sets up an opposition between active, vigilant reason and the passive, routine tradition. Critical theory is not called "critical" because it abounds in critical consequences, but because it considers that a rational approach to human mores dictates that one criticize the existing mores through an application of the transcendental norms provided by reason. For a critical theorist, human minds still need to be liberated from the errors under which they labor: most human beliefs remain mired in superstition, almost all social institutions have been based on arbitrary distinctions, and human relations are too frequently nothing more than relations of domination. Baudelaire, on the other hand, shows that the *thundering reason* invoked by revolutionaries has its own blind spot: "The Revolution, through sacrifice, confirms superstition."[41] In other words, no Philosophe will ever be able to reason out the spectacular rite of the guillotine, chief tool of the Revolution.

A Baudelairean philosophy of modernity takes the opposite posi-

---

39. Baudelaire, "The Painter of Modern Life," p. 392 [translation modified].

40. Ibid., pp. 396–97 [translation modified].

41. Baudelaire, "Mon coeur mis à nu" (no. 6), p. 631.

tion: well-established customs have their own legitimacy, commonly shared beliefs are not without their raison d'être, and human relations are never simple relations of force. Baudelaire has a different notion of rational justification than the rationalist philosophers. For there is no place in critical theory for the idea of a *legitimate and mysterious reason for all customs*.

=4=

The French Crisis of Enlightenment

In *The Philosophical Discourse of Modernity*, Habermas advances a stern critique of one current of French thought, one on which he bestows the odd name of "neostructuralism." In fact, Habermas has it in for authors like Bataille, Derrida, and Foucault who belong, according to him, to a certain French Nietzschean legacy. In order to situate this current within the general line of the philosophical discourse on modernity, Habermas draws up a table of the philosophical possibilities available at the time of Hegel's death. In it he derives a third Hegelian possibility in addition to the already well-established Old Hegelian (rightist) and Young Hegelian (leftist) schools.

Young Hegelians see themselves as an avant-garde: they have great expectations for the future because, as they say, the real of today does not satisfy the rational demands of individuals. The Old Hegelians also find the present to be lacking: "civil society" is atomized, existence is fragmented, and the individual consciousness insists on being recognized in its singularity. Nevertheless, the Old Hegelians regard these shortcomings as the necessary concomitants of humanity's having reached adulthood. They expect religion and the State to educate those individuals who remain too closely tied to "immediacy." In their view, the just requirements of a reasonable mind have already been satisfied.

But a third line of thought has recently come to advance a somewhat startling view: the real is to be criticized not because it is lacking in rationality, but precisely because it is already *too* rational. Habermas portrays Nietzsche as the originator of this philosophical heresy whereby the real is the rational and for that "reason" must be denounced. He then has little difficulty showing that one cannot both take a critical stance (i.e., give *reasons* against something) and at the same time speak in the name of something other than reason.

Between the two traditional alternatives, the Nietzschean heresiarchs would form a third party, advocates of neither *order* nor *movement*, but of the *unjustifiable*. By turns this new faction will proclaim itself to be Dionysian, surrealist, deconstructive, postmodern.[1]

The amazing thing is that this audacious depiction of things is not inaccurate with regard to the French authors in question (I'll say nothing of Nietzsche, who seems to me to have been somewhat mistreated by Habermas). Immediately before the war, French philosophy (or perhaps one should say: the young philosophers and intellectuals of the Parisian avant-garde) received a powerful injection of Hegelian themes. In this context, one should mention not only Alexandre Kojève's course, but the role of the genuinely Hegelian philosopher Eric Weil, as well as the interest in the young Marx, in Kierkegaard, and in Heidegger aroused by *Recherches philosophiques*, a journal attentive to German philosophical currents.

What is troublesome is the facility of Habermas's *immanent* critique. It is accurate to see Hegel as the philosophical point of departure for a certain line of French thought. Though Habermas is certainly wrong to number Nietzsche himself among Hegel's heirs, he rightly perceives a certain Hegelian reasoning *gone wild* among Nietzsche's French interpreters. What gives this line of thought its particular flavor is not its would-be "neostructuralism" but its explosive mixture of dialectics and "philosophy with a hammer." Habermas takes pains to remind his readers that Nietzsche is not easily classed among writers who could be considered leftists. He quite effectively criticizes the

---

1. It is unfortunate that Habermas did not devote any of the chapters of his book to the work of Jean-François Lyotard. Of all the French authors targeted by Habermas, Lyotard's references (Marx, Freud, Adorno, linguistic philosophy) are closest to those of Habermas himself. The difference in their positions is thus all the more significant.

contradictions and ambiguities implied by a Nietzscheanism of the extreme left ["un nietzschéisme rouge"]. But it would have been still more accurate to speak of a dark Hegelianism ["un hégélianisme noir"]. Beyond the French authors taken up by Habermas, one would have to include Klossowski and Blanchot in this "melan-Hegelian" line, if only for their interpretations of Sade and Lautréamont. Lastly, it is to be noted that even Deleuze was so preoccupied with escaping the ambient melan-Hegelianism of the time that he ended up appearing as a kind of anti-Hegel—yet another symptom of the Hegelian mania.

Habermas does not concern himself with whether, in the period from approximately 1930 to 1960, there might not have been real reasons for French minds to be disturbed. Ever faithful to the rules of immanent critique, he contents himself with the easy task of showing the French authors in question to be in contradiction with themselves. What he does not seem to realize is that his objections have lost some of their force, for the simple reason that they have already been raised by orthodox Hegelians like Eric Weil, precisely in the name of reason defined as nonviolent dialogue. Indeed, the heresiarchs of Hegelianism have already been *corrected* several times by various masters. But they have demonstrated an almost diabolical intransigence that it behooves us to try to understand.

Here one cannot avoid examining what can only be called the French crisis of Enlightenment. Habermas is quite right to point out that the ideas of the French authors cited above have German origins. But a strange inversion is produced as a result. Habermas has appropriately set himself up as a sort of conscience among German intellectuals (or rather, among the German professoriat). In this capacity he deplores the absence of a vigorous tradition of critical thought in these milieus, reproaching his compatriots for not having given the *Aufklärung* enough of a chance and for having been too quick to abandon the modern project. Yet this sort of reproach cannot be leveled at the French in the same terms. There certainly has been no shortage either of French intellectuals and professors committed to the left, or of antifascist organizations. The perplexities of the French case spring from a different source.

To put it in somewhat overly general terms, we in France do not reason within the perspective opened up by a modern *project*. Rather, our thinking is determined by what one might call a modern *accomplishment*. We do our thinking in the wake of our Revolution, the legacy of which deeply unites us even before dividing us from one another.[2] And this can only mean one thing: *we reason in the wake of the (French) Revolution's failure to liberate humanity*. The temerity of this sentence indicates only that we are not concerned here with historical facts *tout court*, but with those of them that can be accommodated within French political lore or accepted by the French civil religion. How does the collective system of representations that allows the French to identify themselves as *French citizens* reconcile itself to the obvious discrepancy between the revolutionary promise and the post-revolutionary experience? This discrepancy, which continued to take shape right up until World War I, was already recognized at the time. And the most lucid of its contemporary observers drew the sociological conclusion that the social cannot be manufactured through political operations. This double failure brought with it a double disappointment. In the nineteenth century there first appeared the phenomenon of *nationalism*, followed at the turn of the century by the burgeoning possibilities of *populist demagogy*. Neither of these should be viewed as a regression, as a falling back into a previous formation, but as the "misfortunes of democracy."[3]

In what way is there a specifically French crisis of Enlightenment? When they shouted "Vive la Nation!" at Valmy, the French had no inkling that they were inaugurating the age of national wars. In French thought the *principle of nationalities* is first and foremost an idea of the left, an ideal of liberation that will put all peoples on an equal

---

2. What I mean by this that those among us who do not see the Revolution as having played *any* role in what makes them French are either too eccentric or too muddleheaded to really participate in public debate in France.

3. The expression is that of Louis Dumont: *Homo Hierarchicus: The Caste System and Its Implications*, trans. Mark Sainsbury, Louis Dumont, and Basia Gulati, 2nd ed., (1970; rpt. Chicago: University of Chicago Press, 1980), p. 15. He elaborates on this point by saying that any reflection on modern democracy "evidently ought to consider the *whole* of the history of the modern democratic universe, including on the one hand the wars, and on the other the Second Empire, the Third Reich or the Stalinist regime" (p. 347n.).

footing. When Napoleon III went to war with Austria to bolster the cause of Italian unity, the Parisian populace surprised everyone by its demonstration of enthusiasm. As Emile Ollivier, a liberal who was at that time a member of the opposition, tells it:

> In working-class districts the enthusiasm bordered on delirium; at the place de la Bastille, the crowd hurled itself at the Emperor's car, frantically waving their caps and shouting, "Long live the Emperor, long live Italy, long live the army!" This surprised friend and foe alike. The passion of the French democracy for the emancipation of other peoples had manifested itself once again. Even those who, since December, had shown no enthusiasm for the emperor of the coup d'état, now championed the emperor in war. The people of Paris had none of our scruples, nor did they emulate us by abstaining: they warmly approved the emperor, lining up behind him rather than behind the deputies he had expressly named to make up the opposition.[4]

Thus, the emancipation of national populations is of a piece with the progress toward a general brotherhood of man that also brings with it the abolition of social inequalities, the redemption of work, and so on. In the course of the century, the nationalist idea gradually migrates from the left to the right. By General Boulanger's time, an intellectual who saw himself as opposed to chauvinism and unwilling to accept the nationalist "hysteria" of the people either had to put his faith in the future evoked by a socialist international, or get used to thinking outside the existing *consensus* between the people and their leaders, in the same sort of solitude that Nietzsche had to endure after 1870.

According to popular opinion, World War I was the result of a conflict of nationalisms. Those in the minority, who had cast their lot with what they saw as the underlying internationalism of the working masses and their organizations, had egregiously miscalculated. Nevertheless, thanks to the defeat of the Russian Empire and the separate peace, it was possible to rescue the ideological certitudes of the French. Afterward the conflict came into clear focus: the democracies would vanquish the empires, and the principle of nationalities would thereby be returned to a place of honor. There was no

---

4. Cited in Jean Plumyène, *Les nations romantiques* (Paris: Fayard, 1979), p. 240.

longer any reason to doubt that the empires defeated in the war had been condemned by history. It went without saying that the new map of Europe—a map from which Musil's anachronistic monster of "Kakania"[5] had been effaced—was more *modern*, and thus more viable, than the old one.

But the peculiarly democratic misadventure known as "world war" is inseparable from another calamity of the Enlightenment: the formation of *masses*, and the political exploitation of this phenomenon through Leninist and fascist techniques of political organization.[6]

For liberal thought, the human ideal would be to expand what one might call an *ecclesiastical* social structure—that of the first Christian communities—to all aspects of life. Such a structure consists in a maximal reduction of all relations of an institutional sort. Accordingly, there would be neither masters nor slaves, men nor women, parents nor foreigners. All human relations would be informal and familiar, as it should be among *brothers* (or among *comrades*). Something of this kind is anticipated within egalitarian sects, whether born of transcendent religions or of millenarianism (and here I am thinking of the "cadres" and "active minorities" of the revolutionary movement). Thanks to the annulment of institutional differences, a kind of intense human kinship and felicitous liberty of purely personal relationships comes to flower. Institutions no longer predetermine who one is and in opposition to whom, and nothing from outside comes to disturb the purely human relation between one person and another. This ideal is a concentrated version of the individualist utopia: a human group constituted by purely ethical relations among individuals (and by "ethical relations" I mean relations governed by the personal conscience of each individual and not by some instituted order over and above the individuals).

It is therefore profoundly disturbing for anyone brought up in such a liberal perspective to observe the wholly modern phenomenon of *crowd*

---

5. Translator's note: "Kakania" is a term Robert Musil uses to refer to the Austro-Hungarian monarchy. See his *Man Without Qualities*, trans. Eithne Wilkins and Ernst Kaiser (New York: Coward-McCann, 1953).

6. Today the word "socialism" is often used to designate little more than this manipulation of the populace by a mass party apparatus.

formation. Nowadays one speaks of *masses,* but *Massenpsychologie* derives from the "psychology of crowds" developed by Gustave Le Bon with regard to the stories told about Parisian mass movements during the Revolution.[7] The people within a crowd change their "psychology": outside of the crowd they are well balanced and sensible; within it, they become gullible, emotional, and irascible. Their "emotions" are no longer under the control of "reason" and must be discharged immediately, in a "primitive" or "puerile" way, through shouts, gesticulations, and "magic" violence committed against symbols and scapegoats. The *critical mindset* is placed in suspension: the crowd believes the most unlikely sorts of information, changes its opinion at the drop of a hat, and allows itself to be guided by mere slogans instead of rallying around the better argument.

Along with the agitated human throng and its threatening *tumult,* another character comes into play: the demagogue. Out of the crowd a *leader,* a *meneur,* a *Führer* comes to the fore. All the duly appointed authorities have lost their credibility and are no longer able to make themselves heard. The traditional leaders have fallen out of favor. All order has disintegrated when out of the general chaos emerges the *strong man* who issues commands, identifies the guilty parties, and gives order to the mobilization of energies.

In order to understand this feat, theorists of various stripes have looked to every possible natural scientific model of action at a distance, or the rapid propagation of movement. The formation of the crowd has been variously theorized according to the models of *epidemic contagion,* of *energetic fields* (the crowd is described as electrified, magnetized, galvanized), of collective *hypnosis* (or suggestion), and of *animal mimetism* (the gregarious behavior of the herd). But for liberal thought, the problem is not so much one of explaining the phenomenon by means of some mechanism as it is one of understand-

---

7. The bibliography on this subject—from Gustave Le Bon, *The Crowd: A Study of the Popular Mind* (New York: Penguin, 1960), to Elias Canetti, *Crowds and Power,* trans. Carol Stewart (New York: Continuum, 1973), by way of Georges Sorel, *Le procès de Socrate* (Paris: F. Alcan, 1889), and Sigmund Freud, *Group Psychology and the Analysis of the Ego,* in *Standard Edition,* trans. James Strachey (London: Hogarth Press, 1955), vol. 18—is immense. I found the overall view offered in the work of Friedrich Jonas, *Geschichte der Soziologie* (Hamburg: Rowolt, 1969), III, 7–29, to be quite useful.

ing its very possibility within the liberal philosophical conception of history. How are we to understand the fact that, in the modern age, individuals who had hitherto behaved as autonomous human beings, each one responsible for himself, should spontaneously come to renounce their autonomy in order to return to a more "primitive" state of humanity? How can an individual tire of being autonomous? The fact that he does so calls into question the whole idea of an evolutionary progression running from "closed" societies to "open" ones. According to this latter view, "primitive" societies are *closed* in a way that does not permit individuals to think for themselves, to distinguish themselves from others, or to retreat from the society. On the other hand, "civilized" societies are *open*: they disapprove of gregarious comportments and approve of independent qualities among their members. With this schema, the liberal theory of history willingly admits that sociologists have much to say about primitive tribes and still more about complex traditional societies (like India, China, or Japan). They can even analyze the European feudal system. But sociology ceases to be valid once one moves from archaic Greece to consider classical Greece: for in such a case one has moved from *mythos* to *logos*! All the more reason why notions like "collective consciousness" and the "opposition of the sacred and the profane" cannot be applied to contemporary Western societies.

As for what concerns us here—the limitations of the conception of human life within the more or less official philosophy of the Third Republic—the important point is that no compromise can undo the setback suffered by the liberal philosophy of history. It is useless to talk of regression, relapses into the primary processes of the psyche, or the reappearance of humanity's primitive traits. For a liberal thinker, the disappearance of traditional social orders in the modern age *ought to* bring with it the liberation of the individual. Conversely, the formation of the crowd *ought to* mark a return to a tribal stage of humanity. Yet this is not at all the case. The dissolution of the social order did not give birth to sovereign individuals, but rather produced a deep disorder against which the social body reacted violently as a way of defending itself. And yet, contrary to the expectations of critical rationalism, the rise and establishment of the new totalitarian order does not represent a return to any sort of *holistic* form of organization. Rather, it marks the constitution of something *ultramodern*: the fabrication of a collective identity out of representations like "class struggle" or "race war" that are its own negation.[8]

Again, my focus here is not the history of the twentieth century, its wars, totalitarian regimes, or the global impact of the European conflict. Nor is it the set of events that make up our age; rather, my topic is the philosophical response to those events and is thus both limited and precise. My subject is not even the well-documented moral disarray of French society before and after the last war. Historians will be able to provide a necessarily complex explanation of the French decline; complex in that it will have to mention the enormous losses in World War I, the decline in population, the ineptitude of the leaders, the political divisions, and so on. But this moral disarray has been accompanied by an *intellectual* disarray, one that arose at that time and has not been truly overcome since. And this is precisely the place for the reflections of a philosopher intervening *as* philosopher.

It is commonly assumed that the civic function of intellectuals is to "think the event." More often than not, this amounts to providing a moral identity to whatever happens, and doing so *in the language of the civic creed* of the society: that is, in a language understood by everyone and that prepares the community for the difficult choices that this event may require. Only events entailing neither personal nor collective decisions can be described in purely physical terms or in a neutral vocabulary. But if our group is compelled to react, then the recent or impending change in the state of things must be described to us in a language that clearly delineates responsibilities and merits, duties and rights, in such a way that the event comes to mean either threat or relief, victory or defeat, crime or punishment. In the utopia dreamed of by rationalist philosophers, each individual, in his capacity as a thinking being, has access to the same universal vocabulary that must be used if an informed decision is to be reached. This vocabulary will be used in the free formation of public opinion through communication among individuals. The philosopher's job, then, becomes one of

---

8. See Louis Dumont's study of the "totalitarian disease" translated by Paul Hockings and Louis Dumont as chapter 6 of his *Essays on Individualism: Modern Ideology in Anthropological Perspective*, (Chicago: University of Chicago Press, 1986).

rendering explicit the vocabulary of human reason and making sure that this vocabulary is the one used in public discussions.

But all this amounts to the purest philosophism. The only thing one can ask of the philosopher is that he not limit himself to the role of watchdog over a system exemplary in its "rationality" and internal coherence. He must also, if the occasion arises, be sensitive to the irrational aspects of the system. At that point, the critical task carried out by true philosophers is one of acknowledging the intolerable paradoxes resulting from the uninformed use of the vocabulary in force, so as to work toward their solution. In other words, there is necessarily a certain local and contextual quality to the most important conceptual revisions.

In 1938 a truly philosophical problem arose for anyone who seriously took stock of the following fact: democratic regimes seemed at that time incapable of mobilizing the energies of their citizens for the defense of what they held to be most sacred. At the same time, regimes that were clearly tyrannical were enjoying the greatest success in this same endeavor: these regimes approached the test of strength, which everyone at that time saw looming, in the best possible state of material and spiritual preparation. I am not concerned here with the relevance of this assessment, which one might feel inclined to revise in light of what followed. For example, everyone in France seems to have overestimated the capabilities of the fascist regime in Italy, and no one foresaw the role that the United States would come to play in the conflict. My concern here is the philosophical problem that necessarily arises when one admits that the 1938 diagnosis of the situation was at least partially correct, that it reflected the respective situations in France and Germany at that time. Moreover, what is philosophically thought-provoking is the very possibility that the 1938 diagnosis *might* be correct, that it cannot be dismissed as absurd in advance, that the unhappy situation it describes is not *logically* inconceivable. For if the diagnosis in question is not a contradiction in terms, the following problem arises: How are we to explain the fact that a *people*—what we designate with the noble name of "people"—had become inspired by the inhuman ideals of an openly tyrannical regime, at the same time that another people, under a democratic regime, became demoralized? The problem is a philosophical one, for to come to terms with the very *possibility* of this fact requires a partial and radical revision of the conceptual framework that organizes our collective view of things. "Is Hitler supported by the German people?" This is a question of fact, one to be decided through political and historical judgment. "Is it even conceivable that a tyrant could be popular, that his people could be mobilized behind him rather than against him? Isn't this situation, despite the fact that it is impossible according to our civic creed, a very real possibility in our world?" Here we have a conceptual, philosophical question (and it should go without saying that every historian asks both sorts of questions: questions of fact and conceptual questions).

The state of the world now is very different from what it was in 1938. In order to recapture the general atmosphere before the war, even older readers will still have to supplement the memories of their childhood with the memoirs and historical works of others. Yet the fact that there are no longer any fascist regimes, and that proletarian political parties are no longer enthusiastically received, does not mean that the matter is entirely settled. The intellectual disarray in France did not end with the end of the war. In my opinion, the war has continued to determine the *tone* and *mood* of intellectual debate in France right down to the present day. Indeed, it seems as though the intellectual revisions that seemed to be imperative in 1938 have been indefinitely and continually postponed, first on account of the war and its demands, then because of the need for reconstruction (which, as everyone knows, only really came to an end with the settling of the colonial question under the Fifth Republic). The debate of 1938 was not taken up again in 1945. Perhaps it could not have been. The unexpected results of the war fixed for years to come not only the boundaries of the European states, but the political judgments of the Europeans as well. After the war the correct ideological terms in which to describe it were never settled on, for such terms would have had to account for not only the German defeat, but the advent of the cold war as well. Thus neither of the two moral descriptions that one could have given to the events of 1939–45 managed to carry the day. Did the war represent the final confrontation between the fascist and antifascist camps? In that case one would have to give the liberal democracies a lower rank on the ideological scale, since they could only be viewed as less *advanced* than the socialist democracies. By this view, liberal democracy filled the somewhat dull role of the "centrist" or "moderate" among the "united left." But what if one took the war to be a confrontation between democracy and totalitarianism? In that case the great conflict had not found a military solution, leaving the world in a state of instability.

In France, the first version of the event was initially the most widely accepted among intellectuals. After the war Marxism enjoyed an astounding intellectual authority, perhaps because it provided the easiest way to patch up the republican legend about the Revolution. The existence of wars could then be traced back to imperialism, the rise of fascism could be explained by the economic crisis and the cynicism bred by advanced capitalism, and anti-Semitism could be seen as the sort of irrational conviction to be expected among a bourgeoisie whose historical mission was a thing of the past.

It was only in the 1980s that the second version won out over the first. Today, the idea that there is an antithesis between democracy and totalitarianism is accepted by most people in France where, twenty years ago, it had been rejected as an American fabrication. At the same time the rallying cry is no longer "Power to the workers!" but "Human rights!"

I believe it would not be difficult to find the sort of scenario that I have sketched out here underlying many of the recent debates among French intellectuals. It is as if a *trauma* had been unleashed on the French psyche before the last war, requiring a continual reenactment of the original scene in all its versions until an acceptable resolution was found. It also strikes me as being of little use to find the key to the nihilism of post-Sartrian French philosophy in that philosophy's current political positions.[9] The youth revolt of 1968 can neither serve to explain nor be explained by the structuralism and poststructuralism that followed. Authors like Althusser, Foucault, and Derrida (to say nothing of Lacan, who is often described in this context as a philosopher *honoris causa*) were in no way theoretically equipped to anticipate the ideas of May '68. They were even less able to approve of such ideas. To

---

9. Luc Ferry and Alain Renaut have done so in their recent book, *French Philosophy of the Sixties: An Essay on Antihumanism*, trans. Mary H. S. Cattani (Amherst: University of Massachusetts Press, 1990).

my mind, an explanation for the tone—by turns one of desperation, cynicism, indifference, and outright fiendishness—of the authors of this "generation" (and I mean by this an "intellectual generation" as defined by the public, rather than by the age of its members or the dates of their publications) should be sought less in the ten years of Gaullism and the rise of the human sciences than in the formative experiences of their adolescence and childhood. The rapid succession of political regimes, each one demanding obedience to its laws and accusing the others of illegitimacy, does not make plausible the notion of *consensus*. The moral order invoked by the Vichy government partly explains why some have felt a desire to place themselves "beyond good and evil." The experiences of the black market, of anonymous accusations and the vagaries of the prosecution of collaborationists after the war, could not but awaken an interest in the "microphysics of power."

It is difficult to read the minutes of the June 17, 1939, meeting printed in the *Bulletin* of the French Philosophical Society (40th year, no. 2) without being moved. The members of the Society who went to hear Raymond Aron develop an argument entitled "Democratic States and Totalitarian States" were unaware that the activities of their association were about to be interrupted and would not resume until 1945. In fact, the full text of Aron's lecture only appeared in the 1946 volume of the *Bulletin*. On the back cover of the last issues published in 1938, one finds several advertisements for the Armand Colin publishing house. In one, on the back cover of the first issue in 1938, the following announcement is printed:

> *Just published*: Albert RIVAUD (Professor at the Sorbonne and the Ecole des Sciences Politiques), *The Resurgence of Germany, 1918–1938*.

The text of the announcement reads as follows:

> If any books are relevant to current events, this work by Albert Rivaud is foremost among them. . . . Propelled by National Socialism, the Third Reich has become an immense army seeking to live solely from the resources provided by its own territory. Hitler has managed to impose on the fanatical masses a dictatorship of the most capable technicians resulting in a shocking alliance of dema-

goguery and technology that may continue for some time. But this
system is incompatible with the existence of other nations. It is thus
incumbent upon those nations to defend themselves, both through
internal reforms assuring their unity and strength, and through specific military and economic agreements that address the looming
threat of conflict.

The back cover of the sole issue of the *Bulletin* published in 1939—an
issue containing papers by Jean Cavaillès and Albert Lautman[10] on
"mathematical thinking"—informs us that Rivaud's book is in its
fourth printing and has received various prizes. Thus even within the
austere organ of the French Philosophical Society one can hear the
growing noise of the outside world and feel the concern mounting with
every reedition of a book whose blurb reveals everything that is unacceptable about the current state of affairs. An ordinary reader of the
Bulletin could not help but be outraged to learn that Hitler's project
had encountered no massive internal resistance and that all Germany
had been mobilized and made to function as an army. One should also
note how much more appropriate is the blurb's evocation of the
"shocking alliance of demagoguery and technology" than Heidegger's
famous description of Nazism as "the encounter between global technology and modern man."[11] As much as Heidegger was willing to
describe in copious detail the metaphysics of technology and its
Parmenidian presuppositions, he remained notably silent about topics
like demagoguery and dictatorship. Indeed, the highly abstract Heideggerian notion of *Mobilmachung* [mobilization] calls to mind some sort
of concentration of energy for projects on a global scale; it has lost all
of its military and civic connotations. And to speak of "modern man"
in the singular does nothing to make the examination of relations
among men in the plural any easier.

In his lecture Aron set himself the task of untying the conceptual knot
that had paralyzed the French understanding of totalitarian regimes. As
was customary, he distributed in advance a text containing eight propo-

---

10. Both men took part in the Resistance during the German occupation and both
were assassinated by the occupying forces.

11. Martin Heidegger, *An Introduction to Metaphysics*, trans. Ralph Manheim (New
Haven, Conn.: Yale University Press, 1959), p. 199.

sitions to be developed. Among these propositions, numbers 5 and 7 were perhaps the most difficult for the audience to listen to.

> 5. *Totalitarian regimes are authentically revolutionary; democracies are essentially conservative.* . . .
>
> 7. *Everywhere the political and historical optimism of the nineteenth century is dead.* Today it is not a matter of rescuing the illusions of the bourgeoisie, of humanitarians or pacifists. The outbreak of irrationalism in no way disqualifies the necessary attempt to question progressivism, abstract moralism, and the ideals of 1789. Quite the contrary. Democratic conservatism, like rationalism, can only be redeemed by renewing itself.

These two theses could be said to reveal the "sore spots" [*points de douleur*] of the progressive mindset.[12] A first sore spot is to be found in the zone containing the enthusiasm for the Revolution. A second sore spot is located in the place where perfectly abstract moral judgments are issued in the name of the "ideas of 1789."

By suggesting that revolutions are not necessarily liberating, and that democratic institutions are worth conserving, Aron was fulfilling his duties as a philosopher. He showed how things that are indissoluble in our common consciousness are not for that reason necessarily indissoluble *conceptually*. And here Aron struck the first "sore spot": for any French person, with the possible exception of those few raised in some sort of clerical ghetto, the word "revolution" suggests something eminently worthy of respect and pride, the very historical mission of our country. Aron was asking his audience not only to accept the fact that revolutions can fail or be corrupted, but also to completely revise the concepts through which they thought about the idea of revolution. For without such a conceptual revision, certain historical facts would always be held to be mere accidents or exceptions. For example, the French have all learned, as a matter of historical fact, that the Empire followed the Republic. Nevertheless, the phenomenon whereby social upheaval results in concentrated power is not deemed to be significant. This blind spot in

---

12. I use the phrase "sore spots" [*points de douleur*] by way of analogy with what François Roustang has described as the "point of horror" [*point d'horreur*] and the "point of laughter" [*point de rire*] that are part of any reading when pushed to its limits: "On Reading Again," in *The Limits of Theory*, ed. Thomas M. Kavanaugh (Palo Alto, Calif.: Stanford University Press, 1989), p. 129.

the republican legend prevailing among philosophy professors of the Third Republic is what a sociology of revolution should be concerned with.[13] It is apparent that this problem in vocabulary—are we to describe the Nazis as "revolutionaries"?—cannot be reduced to a mere dispute about words. What is at issue is the very moral identity of the events. If one starts out by maintaining that revolutions are by definition liberating acts, one is logically required to see liberation in every revolutionary movement—in that of Stalin, for example. In other words, one cannot but conclude that such a regime is simply passing through a terroristic phase, and that things will only get better. Inversely, one is also logically obliged to deny the revolutionary quality of social movements that are not also emancipatory. Yet if the Nazi regime is not revolutionary, some kind of conflict—in the form of popular resistance—would have to arise between the leaders and the masses.

A second "sore spot" comes into view when one directs one's gaze beyond the borders of France. In the discussion following his lecture, Aron was chastised for having failed to recognize the importance of the antifascist movement. Those who took part in this movement saw themselves as fulfilling their moral obligation to resist the rise of fascism. Aron's response is the same as the one paraphrased in his *Mémoires*:

> I have said it before: I did not believe in the danger of fascism in France because none of the elements which made up the fascist crisis elsewhere—a demagogue, alienated masses, a will to conquer— were present there. The antifascists were busy chasing after a phantom enemy and thus were unable to to agree about the main issue: the method by which to combat the real enemy—Hitler.[14]

The mindset of the progressives makes it difficult for them to make a distinction between *civil* opposition to the fascistic tendencies of the French extreme right, and *military* opposition to the ambitions of Chancellor Hitler. They find it difficult to admit that one cannot formulate an external politics in the terms of domestic politics. For, to

---

13. *Sociologie de la révolution* is the title of a book by Jules Monnerot (Paris: Fayard, 1969). One might very well have reservations regarding the content of this study (e.g., its excessive Pareto-Burnhamism meant to "irritate the left") and still recognize the intellectual legitimacy of such a project.

14. Aron, *Mémoires* (Paris: Julliard, 1983), p. 209.

admit this would require nothing less than to agree to look beyond our borders at other countries and other peoples for whom France is not necessarily the pure incarnation of humanity. In reality, the progressive mindset prefers to think of all wars as global extensions of a civil war that is no longer conceived as being between any two factions but rather between an antinational bloc and a bloc embodying the coincidence of the particular (the nation) and the universal (the human).

The tendency to think about any and all conflicts in the terms of the legendary Dreyfus affair is typical of this mindset. Emmanuel Levinas tells how, in 1932, at a time when the situation in Europe had again begun to deteriorate, Léon Brunschvicg asserted that "the members of my generation had only been victorious twice: in the Dreyfus affair and in 1918." Brunschvicg went on to add that "now the two battles then won are again on the verge of being lost."[15] But the Dreyfus affair provided a perfect example of a situation where the decision to be made was of perfect clarity precisely because it was plainly a case that required the subordination of political to moral judgment. Nevertheless the Dreyfus affair, which has been taken by French intellectuals as the paradigm for all affairs and which serves them as a model of the judgments to be passed in the face of current events, is an exceptional episode. For there were simply no *valid* political reasons for being either *for* or *against* the reconsideration of the case. This is not to say that the affair was without political background or political consequences. A sensible Dreyfusard has no difficulty accepting that the affair had a political side to it, that some Dreyfusards were not so much supporters of Dreyfus himself as they were opponents of his opponents. Defenders of Dreyfus know, or can imagine, that political careers and ministerial alliances were at stake. For them, none of that counts for much where one is able and, indeed, obligated to isolate the appropriate principle. Yet the great crises of conscience of the period between the wars—the invasion of the Rhineland by German troops, the Spanish civil war, the Munich accords—have done nothing so much as to underscore the limits of what Aron, speaking before the Philosophical Society, called "abstract moralism, or the ideas of

---

15. Cited by Maurice Blanchot in "Les intellectuels en question," *Le débat*, no. 29 (1984), p. 18.

1789." Indeed, *principles* no longer provide all that we need in order to choose the right course, for every principle always entails other principles or can be applied in various ways. It is thus impossible not to take into account certain questions that are properly political and which only arise when one considers oneself as belonging to a *group*: Who are our allies? Who are our enemies? What are our real objectives and what are the possible or likely consequences for our community? It is simply impossible to imagine truly political decisions being made anywhere but in this world. They cannot be made by declaring that one is against every faction, against both those in power and their opposition, against every party and against the state, against every-thing currently existing and therefore on the side of values.

Among the signs that the problems of 1938 have remained with us right down to the present day is the recent increase in interest in those prewar intellectual groups that originally posed these problems, most notably the rather strange association known as the College of Sociology.

In the 1960s several motifs borrowed from the College's melan-Hegelian wing were brought back into fashion by a group of writers belonging to the conformist avant-garde. At that time Paris (to say nothing of Cerisy-la-Salle) bore witness to variations running from the sublime to the ridiculous on the themes of *transgression* or *the festival*. If these transgressive exploits seem merely repetitive and futile twenty years after the fact, it is perhaps because the sociological themes that they took as their focus had been entirely emptied of any of the socio-logical content with which Bataille, Caillois, or Leiris had striven to invest them. In the 1960s one simply had to fall in line with the fashionable ideas of the day: an unwieldy alliance of Marxism and Maoism. Yet Caillois, answering the question "What were you hoping to find in sociology?," later remarked:

> It was, I admit, a somewhat anti-Marxist undertaking. Yet this anti-Marxism in no way brought with it any kind of political commitment to rightist ideas. It was just that we were unable to tolerate Marxism's systematic subordination of history to an eco-nomic determinism based on the struggle for life and strictly utili-tarian motivations.[16]

---

16. Roger Caillois, *Cahiers pour un temps* (Paris: Pandora, 1981), pp. 19–20.

One of the unquestionable virtues of the chapter that Habermas devotes to the writings of Georges Bataille is that it is focused on the problems posed by a non-Marxist explication of modern politics. In it, Habermas discusses in some detail Bataille's early essays on fascism and the notion of expenditure. For Habermas, what is at issue is whether the currently prevailing theories, based as they are on the postulate of the *economic* intelligibility of politics, are satisfactory. Should we seek to account for revolutions and the rise of National Socialism using concepts like economic interest, the struggle for control of the means of production, and social classes? To answer in the affirmative is to conceive of human institutions as mere means— means that are perhaps "objectified," "reified," or "fetishized"—that have been put in place by individuals in order to satisfy their drives. This is the anthropological thesis shared by both Marxism and liberalism. By contrast, the sociological thesis of Durkheim and the French School maintains that one must begin by considering world society as a unified whole, a whole that precedes its division into various institutions and antagonistic classes. Throughout his exposition, Habermas makes it clear that he reproaches Bataille not only for his irrationalism of Nietzschean inspiration, but also for his sociological tendencies and Durkheimian premises.

Although Habermas is not wrong to conclude that no satisfactory theory can be built out of the precarious mix of materials and concepts proposed by Bataille, the problem is one of identifying the source of the incoherence. Habermas points out that Bataille's earliest texts relied on a certain Marxist conceptual framework. Through comparisons of Bataille's early work with the ideas of Lukács and Adorno, Habermas concludes that if Bataille had only been able to formulate a Weberian sort of Marxism, he would have been a worthy contributor to the philosophical discourse of modernity.[17]

But it might be more correct to endorse the opposite hypothesis and hold that if Bataille was unable to move beyond the theoretical prejudices of liberalism and Marxism, it was perhaps because he had too much respect for rational philosophy as it was defined to him both by his collaborator at the review *Critique*, Eric Weil, and by Alexandre

---

17. Habermas, *The Philosophical Discourse of Modernity*, trans. Frederick Lawrance (Cambridge, Mass.: MIT Press, 1987), p. 223.

Kojève. Hegelianism, as it was reformulated by these two writers, was at the time considered to be the richest, most intelligent, and the most advanced version of philosophical rationalism. This would explain Bataille's temptation to view the *real* that finds no place in the system of reason as simply *impossible*. But from the moment he began to express himself in Hegelian terms, Bataille was wrong and he knew it. He was condemned to say "nothing"—having put himself in what amounts to a "mystical" position—and was forced to admit to a "culpable" interest in figures of *evil*: sacrifices, ruinous excess, states of fusion and non-discursive communication, tearful fits, insane laughter, poetic ecstasy. One can see it most clearly in the letter he wrote to Kojève in 1937[18]: as a student of philosophers, he knew he was in error; as a rebel against their teachings, he persisted in his antirational meanderings.

Bataille was willing to grant Kojève's thesis: "I grant (as a likely supposition) that from now on history is at its end (except for the dénouement)." The final parenthetical comment would seem to indicate that Bataille was less certain than Kojève of the inevitable victory of Stalinist communism. Nevertheless, according to Bataille, there remains the problem of an incurable human restlessness: in Hegelian terms, a restlessness of the "negativity" of the human being whose nature is such that "it is not what it is and it is what it is not." Since history is all but finished, man can no longer be placated by teleology or millenarianism (or, in Hegeliano-Kojèvian language, by "action"). One can no longer say that man is *not yet* what he must be, or that he is *still too much* what he should not be. After the "end of history" there remains a "negativity without use." As we have seen, this is precisely the position of the third branch of Hegelianism, which holds that men remain unsatisfied even when there is no reason for complaint—no reason rooted in or presentable in a discourse that is constrained to be communicative.

Eric Weil is perhaps the best representative of a posthistorical rationalism, the main thesis of which could be expressed as follows: there is not just reason, there is also the *Other of reason* that can only be

---

18. Georges Bataille, letter to Alexandre Kojève, 6 December 1937, in *The College of Sociology (1937–39)*, ed. Denis Hollier, trans. Betsy Wing (Minneapolis: University of Minnesota Press, 1988), pp. 89–93.

spoken of by choosing reason. This thesis corresponds to the following reflection: of course the real is the rational and the rational, real; but unfortunately this is only the case for those who have chosen to see things this way (i.e., in a reasonable light). Is the will to see things in a reasonable light *itself* rational? Can one explain why it is justified? One can, of course, but only to those who will accept reasons (it being understood that *our* reasons seek to be universally acceptable). One cannot explain it to those who stubbornly insist on not accepting our reasons (and who have no better reasons to offer us). This stubbornness amounts to *violence*. Violence thus exists. It is not mere appearance or an irrational detour on the way to the total realization of the rational, as in naive and dogmatic versions of absolute idealism. As a result, Hegelianism has come to correct itself in a way that is often characterized as "Kantian" and according to which there exists something like radical evil.

In this posthistorical Hegelianism it is as if optimism were maintained from the point of view of reason, but simultaneously swallowed up (or *aufgehoben* [sublated]) within a *logical Manichaeism of sense and non-sense*. The dualism of reason and its Other must be considered logical, because its meaning is determined by its coherence and noncontradiction. The philosopher, the self-proclaimed man of reason, agrees to recognize a "finitude" of reason: the impossibility for reason to ground itself. There is no final reason to choose reason over contradiction. Thus for those who have chosen reason's Other—the "romantics" who have opted to be "culpable" or "mystical"— optimism has the *last word*, but that's all. The last word marks the end of meaningful history, but it is not the end of all existence. The last word only awes those who prize the ability to speak (and one must add: to speak in the forms of "coherent discourse"). Beyond meaningful language, there exists an entire tragic sphere of life about which one can say nothing of substance. Reason's Other, which here takes the form of something like an evil deity, has no real name, or has no name that fits. It can only be spoken of improperly, for language is the language of reason and the will to meaning. Any concept with which one would hope to "identify" reason's Other must fail to do so, for everything that such concepts might have to say about reason's Other is immediately bound by the teleology of reason and meaning.

From a logical point of view, this Manichaeism is characterized by a peculiar use of the concept of alterity. This is in evidence in the very phrase "the Other of reason." According to this phrase, if there is something like reason or sense, there must also be some other thing (and only one) that is unreason or non-sense. Such logical Manichaeism does not take into account the difference between otherness in the sense of *alterum* (the other of the two terms of a couple), and otherness in the sense of *aliud* (the other in an indeterminate sense). It happens that this Latin distinction has disappeared in French and that the French word *autre,* which derives from *alterum,* has taken over the functions of the word *aliud.* But logical Manichaeism employs the word "other" as though it always introduced the opposite pole, as though one could assign to any given term another term (*aliud*) that would be its Other (*alterum*). This results in a dialectic, because the Other of a given term is at once its *negative* and its partner in the opposition. So, for example, the left hand is both the *other* hand from the right hand (the right hand's Other) and that which fills the indeterminate description of nondexterity ("something other than the right hand").

It is worth noting that this apparent dialectic evaporates once one asks the philosopher, as some logicians have,[19] to use a less elliptical phraseology. Philosophers like to speak about "the same" and "the other." But the same *what*? The other *what*? The concepts of identity and difference cannot be employed absolutely, but only relative to a concept. The left hand cannot be reduced to being a thing whose entire being would be exhausted by the simple fact of its being something other than the right hand. It is precisely the other *hand*, the other hand of the same *body*, and so on. Alternatively (and remaining within the terms of a treatise on the philosophy of mind), one is perfectly justified in asking: Of what faculty is one speaking when one invokes the (faculty of the mind that is the) Other of (the faculty of) reason? Is it the imagination? Is it perception? Is it the will? Logical Manichaeism does not allow for such diversity. It assumes that all the faculties that are not reason itself have the (negative) property of being other than

---

19. See, e.g., Peter Geach, *Reference and Generality,* 3rd ed. (Ithaca, N.Y.: Cornell University Press, 1980), pp. 63–64.

reason in virtue of a (negative and determinate) property of being *the* Other of reason. A common feature is needed, a unique determination and original essence by which these faculties are other than reason. And *violence* is the property that explains why these faculties partake of the Other of reason. There is thus a violence to be discerned within the imagination, within perception, within the will, and within emotion. Finally, in Eric Weil's terms, there is a violence in all of nature, not only in the nature that is outside man, but in the nature within the individual. For the Greeks, violence was a constraint exerted on the nature and spontaneous tendencies of a thing. For Eric Weil, violence *is* nature, taking the double form of the material world on the one hand, and the "pathological" element (in the Stoic and Kantian sense) within man on the other.

The best *internal* critique of such logical Manichaeism (to which more than one philosopher has fallen prey) is the reductio ad absurdum realized by Jacques Derrida. This critique is better known nowadays under the name "deconstruction," especially in the field of literary criticism, where exercises in dialectics are somewhat uncommon. In his early work Derrida spoke more of "différance" than of "deconstruction."[20] This word was meant to make clear that his project was to bring to light the "violence" inherent in "reason"'s operations of identification. The quotation marks around *violence* and *reason* in the previous sentence and in what follows serve as a reminder that the philosopher understands these words in a special way: "reason" is the

---

20. A note about deconstruction: in Heidegger's work, the word *Destruktion* (or *Abbau*) refers to a necessary stage in the "phenomenologische Konstruktion des Seins"; the goal of the destruction of the metaphysical conceptuality inherited from the tradition is to reach a foundation in originary experiences: see Martin Heidegger, *The Basic Problems of Phenomenology*, trans. Albert Hofstadter (Bloomington: Indiana University Press, 1982), pp. 21–23. Whenever the word is used outside its philosophical context, as it often is by American literary critics, it ends up referring to a paradoxical method of reading virtually anything that can be considered a "text."

One might be more inclined to follow the practitioners of literary deconstruction in their various "readings," if they did not often give the impression of having themselves introduced the logical Manichaeism into the text at hand. The philosophers of this school would perhaps also be more convincing, if they agreed to make a distinction between the "reason" to which certain rationalist philosophers (Eric Weil among them) refer, and the reason that all of us experience in our ordinary reasonable moments.

Other of violence, and "violence" the Other of reason. If one takes these words in their usual sense—without quotation marks—the dialectic never gets off the ground.

Here the dialectic springs from the fact that the same term ("violence") is to be taken both as the negative of its Other (i.e., of "reason") and as its Other's complementary partner. Thus the opposition between "reason" and "violence" is to be deconstructed by the following line of reasoning: the classical rationalist believes that "reason" can be defined by itself (without its Other). Though he may speak of coherence and the opposition between affirmation and negation, he will be unable to avoid mentioning "violence" in the definition of "reason," precisely because of the opposition between the two. "Reason" cannot be altogether unrelated to "violence"—the Other of "reason"—insofar as "reason" constitutes itself through the exclusion of "violence," as a will to resist "violence." Because "reason" derives all its meaning from *not* being "violence," it has its entire origin *in* "violence"; the *reason* of "reason" is "violence," because "reason" does "violence" to "violence" in choosing (without reason) to be "reason."

Here we see the extent to which the notorious "binarism" of which the structural method used by linguists and anthropologists has been accused should really be sought in logical Manichaeism. Moreover, it was Eric Weil who wrote: "In short, sense, all sense, has its origin in that which is not sense and which has no sense—and this origin is only evident from within the resulting sense, from within coherent discourse."[21] This citation not only sets the terms up in a certain hierarchy (sense has priority because it is the condition of manifestation of non-sense), but also begins to "deconstruct" this hierarchy (by suggesting that sense is only sense by extracting itself from non-sense, which must therefore be recognized as the origin of sense and thus as the *sense* of sense).

Bataille also made use of the conceptual opposition between the sacred and the profane, which Durkheim had made the foundation of the conceptual analysis of collective representations. The sociologist was, of course, most interested in the contrast between the two poles

---

21. Eric Weil, *Logique de la philosophie*, 2nd ed. (Paris: Vrin, 1967), p. 61.

and thereby also in the power of this relation to give rise to others (and thus to organize the categories that make up the collective system of classification). The opposition between sacred and profane is a conceptual one. It is always possible to engage in profane activities on working days precisely because there is a quite distinct set of holidays. If not only holy days, places of worship, and words of reverence, but also dark days, impure zones, and flagrant blasphemies have not been established, then one cannot know which times are merely ordinary, which spaces are profane, and what the vocabulary of daily commerce is.

Bataille believed he had to fall in line with the philosophers. As a way of doing so, he attempted to assimilate the profane realm of existence to the *world of reason* and the sacred realm to the *world of violence*.[22] As a result, violence, like the sacred, is seen as a necessary condition for human life. And the philosopher who opts for reason instead of violence becomes a sort of "ascetic," a "Platonist," an "enemy of life."

In short, for Bataille a conceptual framework borrowed from the philosophy of mind of German idealism serves to translate the great sociological themes of Durkheim and Mauss into phenomenological terms (or into the terms of lived psychology, of "inner experience"). Conceptually, such a mixture could only be unstable. Bataille's thought inevitably met the fate of all romanticisms, as he himself did not fail to notice. In an article on the poetry of William Blake, he explains that poetry cannot take as its aim both "sovereignty" (Bataille's term for what a sociologist would call "individualism") and the "sacred" or "myth." Here Bataille comes close to drafting a sociology of romanticism:

> Blake's mythology generally introduced the problem of poetry. When poetry expresses the myths which tradition proposes to it, it is not autonomous: it does not contain sovereignty within itself. It humbly illustrates the legend whose form and meaning can exist

---

22. During a conference presided over by Eric Weil himself, Bataille admitted to having borrowed the term "violence" from Weil and was afraid that he might not have understood it in the same sense. In response, Weil gave his approval to Bataille's use. See Georges Bataille, *Oeuvres complètes* (Paris: Gallimard, 1976), VII, 422.

without it. If it is the autonomous work of a visionary, it defines furtive apparitions which do not have the power to convince and only have a real significance for the poet. Thus autonomous poetry, even if it only appears to be the creation of a myth, is a mere absence of myth.[23]

Baudelaire once defined literary dandyism as "greatness without convictions." This is precisely the difficulty that confronts Bataille in the modern poets and, first of all, in himself. He wants to pronounce words with the power of myth, but he always speaks only as an individual. The images that come to him and the verses he utters are all his own, for the group has not invested him with any powers. As a result, he never manages to convince even himself of his vision. Bataille thus finds himself in a position threatened by literary dandyism.

Something similar can be seen in the young Caillois, whose contribution to the manifesto of the College of Sociology shows the symptoms of a *political* dandyism: a search for greatness by means of political action carried out in the absence of any collective convictions. It is remarkable to hear Caillois speak of the "fate of individualism," as he does in his essay "The Winter Wind." Toward the end of the last century, he explains, European civilization culminated in a moral and aesthetic individualism. Caillois, like many others, was fascinated by the "great individualists" who effectively seceded from and repudiated the deceptive values of the horde. He goes on in this essay to evoke the great difficulties of the age, not only the failure of economic liberalism and the dangers of the political situation in 1937, but also the disturbing fact that the attempts at a free and sovereign way of thinking have never resulted in an affirmation of life and a sovereign mode of existence. Rather, such attempts have only succeeded in leading some to the edge of insanity and others to take refuge in futile forms of literary play. Caillois set about drafting the charter for what would be an alliance of great individualists, an alliance by which free spirits would no longer be atomized in their opposition to social values. They would use such values to rescue the rebellious spirit itself. They would form a group to mobilize society.

---

23. Georges Bataille, *Literature and Evil*, trans. Alastair Hamilton (1973; rpt. New York: Marion Boyars, 1985), p. 85.

The desire to combat society *as* society governs the constitution of the group. As a structure that is more solid and more condensed, it plans to attack society by trying to establish itself like a cancer at the heart of a more unstable, weaker, though incomparably more voluminous structure. What we see is a process of *sursocialization*. As such the projected community finds that already it is naturally destined to make sacred as much as possible, in order to increase the singularity of its being and the weight of its action to the greatest extent possible.[24]

It is clear that this project of "sursocialization" is in part a response to the circumstances of the time, to the despairing recognition of the lack of reaction and catastrophic indecision on the part of the French when the great test of force was at hand.[25] But there is a contradiction in Caillois's thinking at that time which reveals itself here. Following Tönnies, he avails himself of the sociological distinction between society (*Gesellschaft*) and community (*Gemeinschaft*). For a liberal intellectual, a child of the Enlightenment, history entails the eventual replacement of community by society. Human beings should be united not by their origins (a "closed" society), but by the fact that they all belong as equals to the human species and are connected in the pursuit of reasonable objectives (an "open" society). In other words, everything that was once *social* and traditional should become *political* and rational. This is the order of things that Caillois seeks to invert, calling upon liberated intellectuals to form a *community* that will impart its energy to *society*. Had this disastrous inversion of sociological categories resulted in any sort of action—if, instead of exhibiting political dandyism, Caillois were endowed with the requisite convictions—it would have been nothing short of totalitarian. By definition, a community can only have been either bestowed upon individuals or found by

---

24. Roger Caillois, "The Winter Wind," in *The College of Sociology (1937–39)*, p. 36.

25. In this regard, one passage of the "Declaration of the College of Sociology on the International Crisis," which was issued in 1938 (after the Munich accords), is worthy of note: "The College of Sociology regards the general absence of intense reaction in the face of war as a sign of man's *devirilization*. It does not hesitate to see the cause of this in the relaxation of society's current ties, which are practically nonexistent as a result of the development of bourgeois individualism" (in *The College of Sociology* [1937–39], p. 45).

them. Only a society can be constructed. By inverting this conceptual order, Caillois effectively wrote the program of a *sect*. Indeed, Caillois was well aware of this and said as much: his community is to be the result of a coming together based on "elective affinities." Its members will be both applicants and recruits, as in a club or an academy. But here the goal is not to form a club for intellectuals. The goal—to form an elective community—is a contradiction in terms.

The real sociologists in the College were not fooled. Thus Michel Leiris raised the following crucial objection to Bataille: one cannot both draw one's authority from sociology and recur to a presociological mode of thought. Leiris sets things straight when he writes in a letter to Bataille: "As far as the foundation of an order is concerned, it seems premature in any event, as long as we have not managed to define a doctrine. An order is not founded to produce a religion; it is, on the contrary, in the heart of religions that orders are founded."[26] As for Mauss, he sees in the young Caillois the effects of philosophism. In a letter thanking Caillois for having sent a copy of *Le mythe et l'homme* (published in 1938), Mauss expresses his approval of Caillois's mythological work, all the while condemning his irrationalist philosophy ("probably under the influence of the Bergsonian Heidegger wallowing in Hitlerism"): "As convinced as I am that poets and men of great eloquence can sometimes give rhythm to social life, I am equally skeptical of the abilities of any philosophy—never mind a Parisian philosophy—to give rhythm to anything at all."[27]

---

26. Michel Leiris, "Leiris to Bataille," 3 July 1939, in *The College of Sociology* (1937–39), p. 355.

27. Marcel Mauss, Letter to Roger Caillois, 22 June 1938, in Caillois, *Cahiers pour un temps*, p. 205.

=5=

Epochal Metaphysics

> In the form of information, the powerful principle of
> providing sufficient reason holds sway over all cogni-
> tion and thus determines the present world-epoch as
> one for which everything depends on the provision of
> atomic energy.
>
> Heidegger, *The Principle of Reason*[1]

At one point during his lectures on the principle of sufficient reason in
1955–56, Heidegger invokes the sorts of platitudes published in "illustrated magazines" and other organs of "information." In such sources
one might read, for example, that "humanity has entered the atomic
era." Here is Heidegger's commentary: "Humanity defines an epoch
of its historical and spiritual existence by the natural energy at its
disposal and the pressure such energy brings to bear."[2] Heidegger does
not simply condemn this cliché, so prevalent among the editorialists
and prognosticators of the time; instead, he uncovers its deeper meaning. According to Heidegger, it is not contemporary culture that makes
our age distinctive, but the discovery of a new energy source.
Heidegger here accepts the idea that an epoch—ours, in any case—
may be comprehended in an event that affects above all the relationship between human beings and nature. Not that he has nothing to say
regarding the remarkable mutations that have taken place in our age
outside the realms of science and technology. Indeed, in the course of
these lectures he discusses both abstract art (in order to explicitly link
it to the atomic era) and the cold war (which is also seen as an effect of

---

1. Martin Heidegger, *The Principle of Reason,* trans. Reginald Lilly (Bloomington,
Ind.: Indiana University Press, 1991), p. 124.

2. Ibid., p. 29 [translation modified].

the principle of reason, which is responsible for atomic science, with the difference that here the analysis is driven by the fact that Marxism, insofar as it is a *dialectical* materialism, cannot be conceived outside of Hegelian rationalism). But he never considers the possibility that a historical era—ours or any other—might be better understood through an analysis of the structure of human relations. For him, the relationship between *modern man* and *nature* is prior to human institutions. It should be noted in passing that this priority of the relationship between man and nature over the relationship between man and man is itself a modern one, one to which every conception of *homo œconomicus* recurs. And this is perhaps the bridge over which certain Marxists were able to retreat into Heideggerian positions: within the *topos* of modern technology as the fulfillment of Western metaphysics, they were able to discover new ways toward something like the Marxist primacy of productive forces over relations of production.

Heidegger's argument runs as follows: our age is the atomic age because we have atomic physics and its applications. And where does atomic physics originate? It presupposes a metaphysics. This point would be incontrovertible if one took it to mean that physics, like every science, presupposes a metaphysics of its object of study. The conceptual system and principles used by physics are a metaphysics of nature, in that the examination of this system and these principles is more a matter for philosophical analysis than for physical research. The metaphysics that physics presupposes thus inheres in all discussion of questions bearing on causality, time, space, individuality, etcetera.

Yet Heidegger does not link the present age to a particular metaphysics underlying atomic physics. He does not ask, for example, what it is that philosophically distinguishes the physics that makes possible the utilization of atomic energy from the physics of an age where it was believed that atoms were truly atomic, that is, indivisible. Nor does he ask whether modern science requires a metaphysics of substances rather than a metaphysics of events and processes. Heidegger sets aside the still-particular metaphysics that a philosophy of physics would be, in order to draw a direct link between the atomic age and a metaphysical principle of the greatest generality: the principle of reason.

Heidegger certainly did not invent this way of philosophizing. Before him, attempts were quite frequently made to raise the epoch to the level of a philosophical conception. But Heidegger's approach is so distinctive that it merits special consideration as the only example of what we might call *epochal thinking.*

Philosophers have usually sought their answers to the question "What is the defining idea of our epoch?" in one or another of the domains of what Heidegger dismisses as mere "culture." The defining idea of an age might be, for example, the idea of freedom of conscience, or the idea of happiness. In chapter 3 I cited a text in which Baudelaire makes the claim that one can uncover the philosophical line of thought that most affects or troubles an era by looking at prints depicting the fashions of the time. Such prints form part of the "peinture de moeurs" of an epoch. Baudelaire believed that an understanding of a given age could be garnered only through an understanding of its mores. Historians whose interests go beyond political history share this view. Indeed, all such attempts to comprehend the epoch share an *ethnographic* moment comprising the description of mores and customs, rules and institutions. Epochal thinking, by contrast, eschews everything having to do with mores or ethics. Instead, it seeks to establish a relationship between a particular configuration of human existence and a metaphysical proposition pronounced by a philosopher. Henceforth, the principle of sufficient reason is not to be viewed as merely an idea that Leibniz once had. If it were, this great thinker would take on a demiurgic role. No, this principle is not merely an idea of which Leibniz's readers may or may not have been persuaded. Nor is it, for that matter, simply an idea "in the air" at that time, one that Leibniz merely rendered explicit.

In fact, Leibniz himself occasionally stresses the reasonable aspects of his principle and its connection with everyday notions. For him, these latter are like particular cases of the general idea. In a letter to Arnauld, Leibniz makes a distinction between the commonly held axiom—"nothing happens without reason"—and his "great principle," which he formulates in logical terms: for every true proposition there is a sufficient reason for the truth of the attribution of the predicate to the thing that is its subject.[3] This principle is not limited in

3. G. W. Leibniz, letter to Arnauld, 14 July 1686, cited by Heidegger in *The Principle of Reason*, p. 119; an English translation of this letter can be found in Gottfried Wilhelm

scope to what actually happens, to contingent events, or to the domain of physics. Because it is a logical principle, it is general in scope. This is why Leibniz describes it as his "great principle."

One must therefore be careful not to reduce the principle of reason to the principle of causality, which is only its application to the realm of events. Heidegger aptly evokes this difference when he says that, if there is a principle of sufficient reason, there must also be a sufficient reason for this principle.[4] Each time we speak of these principles, we say "*there is* such a principle (of reason or causality)." That is, we assert its existence. Because this sort of existence is ideal, it is without a cause but not without reason. It has the same sort of existence as do the figures invoked by geometers when they speak of, for example, a line having such and such a property or a plane that meets certain conditions. No kind of causality can be brought to bear in such cases. Yet *something* certainly is posited, and attributed not with physical existence but with a certain sort of Being (a certain *entitas*).[5] And that is all that is required for the principle of reason, if there is one, to be applicable. Within the rationalist school, which is itself based on the principle of sufficient reason, it is held that the principles applicable to all things, whether real or possible, give rise to a methodical analysis that this school calls "ontology."[6] Indeed, this is what is suggested by

---

Leibniz, *Philosophical Papers and Letters*, ed. and trans. Leroy E. Loemker, 2nd ed. (1956; rpt. Dordrecht: D. Reidel, 1969), pp. 331–38.

4. Heidegger, *The Principle of Reason,* p. 11.

5. Translator's note: Throughout this chapter "Being" (with an uppercase *B*) is the translation of *être*, which is here in turn a translation of the German *Sein*. The word "being" (with a lowercase *b*) is likewise a translation of *l'étant* in French, or *Seiendes* in German. In the sense in which Heidegger uses these terms, "Being" refers to that of which individual entities of all kinds partake insofar as they "are," while "being" refers to any such entity itself.

6. Throughout this essay I use the term "rationalism" in its doctrinal sense: a rationalist thinker is a partisan of the principle of sufficient reason; he believes that pure reason is a source of necessary truths. The word is also used in a nondoctrinal sense to refer to a way of looking at philosophical work and its manner of proceeding: to be a rationalist in this sense is to be willing to countenance objections and to take the time either to respond with better arguments *or else* correct one's theses. Jacques Bouveresse understands the term in this sense in *Rationalité et cynisme* (Paris: Minuit, 1984). This conception of the way to philosophize, which is one that I share, I shall call "argumentative thought."

the title of the treatise published by Christian Wolff in 1736: *First Philosophy, or Ontology, a Scientific Exposition of the Principles of All Human Knowledge.* In paragraph 70 of this treatise, Wolff provides an argument that, to his mind, proves the principle of sufficient reason. It is one of the hallmarks of the rationalist school not only to recognize the validity of the principle of sufficient reason *but also* to see it as an ontological principle, a law of Being. These are two sides of the same thesis: there is an ontology because there are principles that hold for everything that is, and reciprocally, there are principles which are absolutely universal because there is an ontology, a science of things *taken in general (scientia entis in genere)* or *as mere beings (seu quatenus ens est,* as it says on the first page of Wolff's treatise).

And here we encounter something remarkable: like the rationalists, Heidegger does not doubt for an instant that *there is* a principle of sufficient reason. The fact that other philosophers may not have known about this principle or may not have accepted it is not something that epochal thought seeks to account for. Rather, it views this fundamental principle of Western metaphysics as one that, though it only came to be *formulated* by Leibniz in the seventeenth century, was at work from the very beginnings of philosophy. The general metaphysics—or ontology—of German Scholasticism thus finds itself legitimized as that toward which all previous philosophies tended, beginning with those of Plato and Aristotle. For in order to be able to reduce a given *time* to the statements about *Being* that are made within it, there must be the possibility of formulating a general ontology.

Heidegger insists that as long as one considers Leibniz's principle in its vulgar formulation (i.e., "nihil est sine ratione," nothing is without reason), one will never understand why it is "great" and "powerful." Leibniz provides another, authoritative formulation (authoritative, that is, within Leibniz's thought), which is the one Heidegger cites: "quod omnis veritatis reddi ratio potest" (that for each truth the reason can be provided).[7] Leibniz calls the principle thus formulated the "principium reddendae rationis." And here we reach the fulcrum of Heidegger's entire commentary. For Heidegger translates this Latin phrase as "the

---

7. Heidegger, *The Principle of Reason,* p. 22.

principle of the reason that must be provided": "*Ratio* is *ratio red-denda*. This means that reason is what must be provided to the representing, thinking person."[8] Heidegger thus accentuates, within the name of the principle, the element of debt or requisition (*principium* RED-DENDAE *rationis*). The reason for each truth *must* be provided. It must be. In other words, Leibniz's principle *requires* of us that we give reason for each truth.

For the remainder of his course, Heidegger no longer purports to be discussing a phrase written by Leibniz that proposes an idea. The principle is no longer a *philosophical proposition* of a sort requiring philosophical justification, either by relating it to other philosophical propositions, or through an examination of its propositional construction. Heidegger does not investigate, for example, whether the Leibnizian principle derives from the logical axiom "predicatum inest subjecto" (the predicate is contained within the notion of the subject), even though, for Arnauld, this was the decisive issue. Heidegger seems to feel that by stressing the fact that *ratio* is qualified by *reddenda*, he has demonstrated that Leibniz's principle was not only a proposition made by a particular philosopher, but *the Word of Being itself*. The principle constitutes an appeal regarding the way we are to think Being. It speaks to us in order to enjoin us to dedicate our thinking to a never-ending inquiry into *why*.

Several of Heidegger's readers not only follow him on this point but go even further. Derrida, for example, writes:

> Beyond all those big philosophical words—reason, truth, principle—that generally command attention, the principle of reason also holds that reason *must be rendered*. . . . The question of this reason cannot be separated from a question about the modal verb "must" and the phrase "must be rendered." The "must" seems to cover the essence of our relationship to the principle, it seems to mark out for us requirement, debt, duty, request, command, obligation, law, the imperative. Whenever reason can be rendered (*reddi potest*), it must.[9]

---

8. Ibid., pp. 23–24 [translation modified]. "Must be provided" is a translation of "zugestellt werden muß."

9. Jacques Derrida, "The Principle of Reason: The University in the Eyes of Its Pupils," trans. Catherine Porter and Edward P. Morris, *Diacritics*, 13:3 (1983): 8 [translation modified].

This last sentence marks the tricky point. *Whenever reason can be rendered, it must*! How are we to explain this shift in modalities? Since when does the mere possibility of something suffice to determine its necessity? This shift is even more astonishing than the so-called ontological proof of God's existence (which moves from "God may exist" to "God necessarily does exist"). For here, in addition to the illegitimate transition from a weak modality to a strong one, there is an excessively personal ("destinal") tenor to the necessity in question. Not only *must* reason be rendered because it *can* be, but this "must" is addressed to *us* (and without our really knowing whether we are called upon to demand that everything justify itself before us, or whether we are the ones who must justify everything before the tribunal of Reason).

It will be argued that the troublesome passage from "can" to "must" is present in Leibniz's text itself. Heidegger avoids this weak argument. Where is there a "must" in Leibniz's text? Every formulation he gives of the principle, in the text at hand and elsewhere, speaks of a reason that *can* be rendered. And it can be rendered in principle, by virtue of the ontological thesis. It is never even implied that our finite understanding *will* be able to discover these reasons (which are nevertheless there). But, one might ask, isn't there an obligation contained in the very name of the "great and powerful principle": *principium* REDDENDAE *rationis*? Though it is true that the verbal adjective in Latin indicates an action to be accomplished and is often used to refer to an obligation or task, it is also just as often used with the weaker meaning of simple possibility.[10]

By his deliberately excessive interpretive translation, Heidegger seems to want to focus our attention on an excess that is in the very thing to be interpreted, namely, Western metaphysics. The immoderacy of metaphysics requires that the translator always choose the mean-

---

10. In their book *Syntaxe latine*, 2nd ed. (Paris: Klincksieck, 1953), p. 287, Alfred Ernout and François Thomas write:

> Weakened, the adjective form of many verbs that end in -ndus marked the simple idea of *possibility* in much the same way as adjectives ending in -bilis: amandus (= amabilis), 'amiable'; horrendus (= horribilis), 'horrible'; miserandus, 'pitiable'; contemnendus, spernendus, 'contemptible'; later, adorandus, exsecrandus, uenerandus, etc. With this value, it is usually encountered as an epithet: Cicero, Ph. 2, 15: "o impudentiam . . . non ferendam!," "intolerable impudence!"

ing that is the most serious, most difficult and most consequential. This kind of precipitous rush to extremes is typical of Heidegger and his disciples. If something (with regard to metaphysics) is presented at first as being possible, it soon comes to be presented as inevitable. It is as if the mere mention of a possibility by a philosopher were taken as a dare by his successors. If there happens to be a philosopher who says that something is possible *in itself* (or for God in His absolute power), another one will come along to claim that it is already possible right now, *for us*. If someone claims that a result is attained *at the limit* of an infinite progression, someone else will come along and say that we must proceed to this limit: what the first presents as impossible, the second presents as all but accomplished.

There is indeed a kind of hubris at work within many areas of modern metaphysics. It is a fact of utmost importance that the greatest thinkers of our age seem to be engaged in a race in which they continually "outstrip" one another. Louis Dumont has pointed out the place of the word *Steigerung* (and of the phenomenon, which he calls "intensification") within the literary and philosophical thought of Germany in the age of Romanticism.[11] It is as if the minds of that epoch were enjoined to perpetually *radicalize* their efforts, to *intensify* their ambitions, and to *transgress* the limits imposed on human finitude by their predecessors. Each of them acts as though his most illustrious predecessor were a rival to be bested through a kind of one-upmanship: a more radical point of departure, a more "original" breakthrough, a more all-encompassing totalization. The historians who narrate these sequences (from Kant to Marx by way of the Idealists, from Husserl to Heidegger by way of Scheler) often adopt this perspective as well. As Louis Dumont insists, the process of *Steigerung* has since come to infiltrate all of European culture. For it is the expression of the vital forces underlying that culture: on the one hand, an individualistic tendency that takes the form of a dangerous exaltation of the author at the expense of both the public and what one might call the previous "literary civility" (which presupposed that one writes so as to be read); on the other hand, a general intellectual situation of intense rivalry among national cultures

---

11. Louis Dumont, "Are Cultures Living Beings?: German Identity in Interaction," *Man*, n.s., no. 21 (1986), p. 597.

(and it is well known that nationalism begins in literature). When one examines the major concepts of German idealism in this light, it is evident that not only is there a movement by which they constantly outdo one another (e.g., *Geist* goes one better than the Ego, Praxis transcends the *Begriff*), but that these concepts are often also attempts to surpass the concepts of other national cultures that have been deemed one-dimensional or narrow: reason as *Vernunft* is more powerful than reason as *understanding*, freedom as *Selbstbestimmung* exceeds freedom as *libre arbitre*, art as the power of *génie* triumphs over art as simple *talent*.[12] In this last case, the circumstances of the *Steigerung* are familiar: according to the title of a work by Herder, it is a question of the *Means of Awakening Genius in Germany* (1767), or in other words, the means of developing a *national* literature independent of the classical French model.[13] The obvious interest of an analysis like Dumont's is that it neither ascribes the stylistic and conceptual eccentricities of the authors discussed to troublesome aspects of their personalities, nor does it level accusations at the "epoch" as a whole. In fact, *Steigerung* is not an individual phenomenon, but a collective one. And the features of literary or philosophical style are thus a proper subject matter for a sociology attempting to analyze numerous interactions: between the individuals within a given milieu, between this milieu and the national culture to which it belongs, between the intellectuals of this country and other national cultures.

But was Leibniz himself already laboring under the imperative to always go beyond one's predecessors in a rush to extremes? Must we, in order to think seriously, read his principle in the light of what his successors have been able to draw from it?

The *hermeneuticist* of philosophical texts believes that one must read in this way. He therefore brackets consideration of Leibniz's principle as the philosophical proposition that it clearly is (even for him),

---

12. Translator's note: Since each of these concepts is tied to a national culture, each of them appears in the language of that culture. Thus, in the original French text, *Vernunft* (reason) and *Selbstbestimmung* (self-determination) are in German, *libre arbitre* (free will) and *génie* (genius) in French, and "understanding" and "talent" in English.

13. See Pierre Grappin, *La théorie du génie dans le préclassicisme allemand* (Paris: Presses Universitaires de France, 1952).

in order to concern himself with something that—philologically speaking—it is not: a *call* to think about Being (to think that everything that *exists* or *has Being* [*l'être*] must thereby also have a *raison d'être* and is thus "destined" by "Being" to be interrogated, dissected, analyzed, and calculated by "reason"). For the hermeneuticist who seeks to define an epoch in metaphysical terms, this call is inescapable. In his view, to treat Leibniz's text as a series of philosophical propositions is at once to shirk one's duty and to fall into the most profound delusion (i.e., believing that one can elude the call of "Being" through philosophical cunning). "The *reddendum*, the demand that reasons be rendered, now speaks, ceaselessly and without possibility of discussion [spricht jetzt unabdingbar und unablässig], across the modern age and out over us contemporaries today [über uns Heutige]."[14]

Why is the demand *unabdingbar* (without possibility of discussion)? Why does it have the character of an "inalienable," "unconditional" injunction with which there can be no compromise or coming to terms? This is a good example of the "hermeneutic circle": whether one likes it or not, there is this unconditional appeal, yet it "is" in the text only if one has first agreed to "hear" it.

All the reasons one might provide for interpreting Leibniz's text "epochally" rather than "argumentatively" are flawed. Are we really to believe that by practicing a sober form of philosophy, one that is assessed solely in terms of the quality of its arguments, we are only showing how little we understand about the violence that stirs our age? Of course this may be the case, but here again possibility and necessity are not equivalent. For we may choose to practice philosophy, *even though* the age is one given to pontification and bluster. By thus avoiding grandiloquence, do we then reveal our own kind of hubris, one which consists in believing that, through philosophical sobriety, we might *settle things down*? Perhaps, but perhaps we also prefer philosophy to the *intensification* of our thought. Perhaps we would rather philosophize than attempt to outdo our predecessors, and for the simple reason that we have philosophical questions to ask: because, for example, we would like to know, despite the hermeneuticist's seductive claims, what the illustrious principle of reason

---

14. Heidegger, *The Principle of Reason*, p. 24 [translation modified].

might have to say, if we read it *philosophically* rather than as some kind of proclamation about the "meaning of Being." We would like to know whether this—belated—principle is what the rationalist claims it is: a necessary principle of all reasoning. We would like to know *why* we require such a principle in order to reason. And if the hermeneuticist replies that by posing such questions we reveal ourselves to be adherents of the principle of sufficient reason, we will again ask him why this should be the case. If he says that by asking *this* particular question—why are we rationalists, if we ask for the reason for the principle of reason?—we have then ourselves accepted the ascendancy of the principle of reason insofar as it underlies the question "Why?," we will stop listening to him. If he seems to be merely crafty, we will recognize him as a sophist. If he claims to be speaking seriously, we will invite him to philosophize with us *before* engaging in the race to epochal radicality. For the main problem—the one with which the philosopher should begin—is precisely one of knowing whether it is necessary to ground "Why" questions in a general principle that would guarantee, *in advance* and beyond every particular case, that one can *always* ask for a truth's *sufficient* reason. If the hermeneuticist really believes that one cannot rightfully ask a particular question ("Why?") until one has proved that the same question can be asked in every possible case, then he is in agreement with the dogmatic rationalist. The hermeneuticist thus falls prey to his own excessive faith in the claims of *metaphysica rationalis*.

Here it is important to take the full measure of what is lost if one chooses the epochal mode of thought over the argumentative one. It is evident that the problem with Heideggerian interpretation is that it hardly makes any mention of the fact that the *ratio* to be provided is *sufficient* or *determinant*; the importance of this fact only emerges if one considers the principle in view of its applications. Indeed, this is the only properly philosophical way of examining a principle; for if it is truly a principle, there is no possibility of *proving* it. Heidegger invites us to study the origins of the principle rather than its applications.[15] But if the meaning of the principle can only be uncovered

---

15. Ibid., p. 59.

through an exploration of its applications, one cannot hope to understand its origin and derivation without first undertaking a closer examination of its uses. It must first be studied in action.

The principle of sufficient reason is most familiar to us as a way of conceiving a totalization of contingent existences within a single world bound up by the *principle of the Best*. It is because Heidegger apparently believes that the ontological version of the principle encompasses all its possible applications—physical, cosmological, theological, moral, etcetera—that he makes no mention of theodicy in his course. Yet this topic bears closer scrutiny.

Leibniz's *Theodicy* deals with a particular sort of existence, namely, contingent existence. But it deals with such existence from the perspective of its justification. Is the existence of a world in which there is evil justified? The rationalist school replies that this world, the existing world, must be the *best of all possible worlds*, by virtue of the principle of sufficient reason. Otherwise, if the existing world were not the best of all possible worlds, if there were not one—and only one—existing world where good (or reality) is maximized while evil (or imperfection) is minimized, if consequently the choice of a world to be produced were not limited to the single *optimum* case, then the first cause of this world's existence would be lacking a reason *sufficient* to have produced *it*, rather than another world or nothing at all.

The *Theodicy* thus bears on contingent existence: not on existence qua existence, but on existence insofar as it is justified. Leibniz writes in the preface to this work that it seeks to resolve a question that *disturbs piety at its source*. The question is: How can one claim that the world is beautiful and just, when iniquities often go unpunished and pain is often undeservedly inflicted? I will call this question "the question of existence" for short. And I will use the phrase "the question of Being" to refer to Plato and Aristotle's inquiries into the meaning of words and phrases like *is, is not, exists, may be, seems to be, becomes, ceases to be*, etcetera. (Because this is a matter of metaphysics and not etymology or philology, there is no need to cite these expressions in the original Greek.) It is obvious that, once it has been characterized in this way, "the question of existence" bears little resemblance to "the question of Being." Yet the only possible philosophical justification one can provide for being a Heideggerian is that one thinks that the question of the "meaning of existence" is contained within the question of the "meaning of Being." For Heidegger was right to refuse to be identified as an "existentialist thinker." Heidegger is the opposite of an existentialist, if one understands existentialism as the subordination—indeed, the grounding—of "the question of Being" in "the question of existence." True existentialists take the position that ontological discussions are pointless insofar as they distract us from what should be our true concern: giving meaning to our lives. It is undeniable that Heidegger takes the opposite approach. By subordinating the "existential" question to the investigation of the "meaning of Being," he makes it clear that the inquiries carried out in the name of *piety* can be taken up in a rigorously philosophical manner through the use of phenomenological description and conceptual analysis. This explains, in Jean Beaufret's view, the lofty status generally accorded to Heidegger: Heideggerian philosophy transcribes in terms of *Being* and *Time* the types of questions that had previously been thought to be the exclusive province of religious meditation. "Its appeal was certainly due to the attempt to situate, within phenomenology and directed by a rigorous analytic, certain fundamental concepts that had hitherto been somewhat complacently monopolized by religious revelation: the concept of the fall, for example, or those of fault or of salvation."[16] A discussion of religious questions may invite confusion in a world where one's religion is usually thought of as the totality of one's *beliefs* regarding such matters as the beyond, God, and spiritual powers. But this is merely the philosophistic view. For theologians, *piety*—which is at the heart of religion understood as virtue—is a matter of *justice* and not of *faith*. Piety consists in paying one's just debt in a world that is itself just. Piety thus presupposes that there is an inherent justice to the world (and before the division of the world into the natural and the human). Impiety is only conceivable if the world is no longer understood to be ordered by a justice more powerful than human initiative.

Among modern philosophers, Nietzsche was best able to delineate the "question of existence" as constituting both the most serious ques-

---

16. Jean Beaufret, "A propos de l'existentialisme" (1945), in his *Introduction aux philosophies de l'existence* (Paris: Denoël-Gonthier, 1971), pp. 41–42.

tion for philosophy *and* an interrogation of our own piety or impiety (this last he calls *nihilism*). In his essay on "Schopenhauer as Educator," he derides the Germans who thought that the news of a German empire founded at Versailles constituted a refutation of "pessimistic philosophy." According to Nietzsche, these people have confused philosophical priorities with journalistic ones.

> People of this sort have lost every last shred of religious and philo-
> sophical conviction, and have exchanged them, not for optimism,
> but for journalism, the wit and unwisdom of the day—and the
> dailies. Any philosophy founded on the belief that the problem of
> existence has been changed or solved by a political event is a parody
> of philosophy and a sham.[17]

Because Nietzsche sees the value of existence as the true problem of philosophy, he grants Schopenhauer an importance that Heidegger rejects. What is strange is that Heidegger asks that we read Nietzsche as though he were Aristotle, as if Nietzsche, unlike Schopenhauer, had raised himself from the religious level of the question of "existence" to the metaphysical one of the question of "Being."[18]

According to Nietzsche, the philosophical question regarding the justification of existence has prompted philosophical responses like Leibniz's optimism or Schopenhauer's pessimism. It has also elicited absurd responses from fraudulent philosophers: "Read the newspaper and you will understand what justifies existence, the goal toward which history has been heading: the founding of a new State!" Here it is clear that the answer one gives to the religious question (and this religion may well be atheistic) immediately determines an order of ends, a scale of values, and a hierarchy of duties. If existence is justified by the founding of the new State, the most noble human duty is service to that State. If there are duties nobler than service to the State, then the meaning of existence will have to be sought elsewhere. According

---

17. Friedrich Nietzsche, "Schopenhauer as Educator," trans. William Arrowsmith, in *Unmodern Observations*, ed. William Arrowsmith (New Haven, Conn.: Yale University Press, 1990), p. 184.

18. Heidegger, "The Word of Nietzsche: 'God is Dead,' " in *The Question Concerning Technology and Other Essays*, trans. William Lovitt (New York: Harper and Row, 1977), p. 94.

to the philosopher-educator, the highest duty that falls to the individual is to liberate his own mind. And he truly is an educator, if he can show how this ideal determines "a new round of duties."[19]

It would not be incorrect to say that the "philosophy of existence" first came into being when Leibniz wrote his *Theodicy*. There he explains that he felt compelled to write the book because the *outward forms of religion*—by which he means *ceremonial practices* and the *formularies of belief*—are no longer sufficient to assure a *sound piety*.[20] At the time when Leibniz wrote this, instituted religions had begun to lose their foundations in the minds of the people: it no longer went without saying that piety—or the debt imposed by justice—must consist in rituals and beliefs that were increasingly accused of being positive and "external," that is, imposed on the individual by the community. There had never been any need to pose the "question of existence" in philosophical terms as long as the *answer* to this question was publicly present in the form of the communal celebration of the religious mysteries of salvation. It arose when it did because the individual had been increasingly left to his own devices in answering the question "How do things stand with our piety?" In a fragment from the same period as "Schopenhauer as Educator," Nietzsche writes:

> Clearly, most people *in no way* consider themselves to be *individuals*; their lives demonstrate this. The Christian requirement, that *each one* keep in view his own bliss and *only* this, is in contradiction with human life in general where everyone lives only as one point among many points, not merely as the pure and simple result of previous generations, but also living only in view of the generations to come. There are only three forms of existence in which man remains an individual: the philosopher, the saint, and the artist.[21]

This text shows how the "question of existence" arises for philosophers because the individualist requirement for personal salvation is no longer

---

19. Nietzsche, "Schopenhauer as Educator," p. 192.

20. Gottfried Wilhelm Leibniz, *Theodicy: Essays on the Goodness of God, the Freedom of Man, and the Origin of Evil*, ed. Austin Farrer, trans. E. M. Huggard (London: Routledge and Kegan Paul, 1951), p. 49.

21. Nietzsche, *Werke*, ed. Giorgio Colli and Mazzino Montinari (Berlin: Walter de Gruyter, 1967), IV, pt. 1, pp. 107–8.

limited to the religious sphere. The "philosophy of existence" is thus an integral part of the age of the disenchantment of the world.

It is not surprising that Nietzsche's response to the "question of existence" inheres, as Clément Rosset has shown, in the "experience of music."[22] Music has always provided the vocabulary that best expresses what philosophers have awkwardly called a person's "attitude toward existence" or his "fundamental project." The *well-tempered* harmonies of the *musica instrumentalis* foster a conception of the correspondence between "temperature" and "temperament," between heaven and heart, between the *musica mundana* and the *musica humana*.[23] To put it another way, music allows us to conceive the reciprocal relations between mood and atmosphere. Among men a particular *Stimmung* is made up of a certain state of mind; in the world, of a certain state of things. For Nietzsche, the experience of music constitutes a cosmic piety independent of every objective pretext and every teleological assumption, for this experience entails a kind of joy that is not impaired by the hypothesis of a *chaotic* universe, a mystical joy (in the same way that "physical" love, in which there is a certain concern for self-preservation, and "mystical" love, which accepts perdition, are opposed to each other).

In the *Theodicy*, Leibniz's thought takes part in this tradition of the *harmonia mundi*. On the threshold of the modern age, it is an attempt to formulate a response to the age-old question of the justice of the world. How can myriad existences together come to make up a world that is beautiful (or in theological terms, a world that confirms the radiant glory of its creator)? Now it happens that the only place where Heidegger touches on these issues is not in his discussion of Leibniz, but in an aside at the beginning of the ninth chapter of *The Principle of*

---

22. "For music occupies the 'nerve centers' of Nietzsche's philosophy, taking the place of everything that, in the systems of others, is called upon to play the role of principle or foundation. Music is the answer to every question and thus at once takes the place of theology, metaphysics, and physics. It is the primary Revelation that imparts adequately and once and for all the meaning, cause, and end to all existence." Clément Rosset, *La force majeure* (Paris: Minuit, 1983), pp. 45–46.

23. In this regard see Leo Spitzer, *Classical and Christian Ideas of World Harmony: Prolegomena to an Interpretation of the Word "Stimmung"* (Baltimore: Johns Hopkins University Press, 1963), pp. 34–35.

Reason, where he cites an extraordinary letter in which Mozart explains his method of composition:

> [M]y subject enlarges itself, becomes methodised and defined, and the whole, though it be long, stands almost complete and finished in my mind, so that I can survey it, like a fine picture or a beautiful statue, at a glance. Nor do I hear in my imagination the parts *successively*, but I hear them, as it were, all at once [gleich alles zusammen].[24]

As an ontological principle that would be the complement of the principle of contradiction, the principle of sufficient reason is somewhat lacking. One would have to be Wolff, or one of his disciples, to really take it seriously. But as a principle of totalization, it allows one to hear the *harmonia mundi* in the same way that Mozart hears—in his imagination—the music of his own compositions: all of the parts *together at once* and not *one after another*. Through this principle, Leibniz attempts to keep alive the possibility of a musical experience of the world, of a world that the sciences of his time had already begun to cut up and dissect in order to explain each part separately, *partes extra partes*.

Now regarding all these features of the "age of the principle of reason"—individualism and the exacerbation of differences, piety and the objections raised by nihilism, the disenchantment of the world as the loss of the music of the universe—Heidegger has nothing to say. Heideggerians see the principle of reason as little more than the proclamation of a kind of generalized calculability, of planning on a planetary scale, of an atomic age. Yet viewed in the light of its cosmological applications, the principle is less modern than they claim. Rather, it is a compromise formulation, an attempt at reconciliation.

Considered as a principle of reason *tout court*, Leibniz's proposition arises out of traditional concerns. Far from being an abrupt assertion of a modern form of rationality that had hitherto been merely latent, Leibniz's idea constitutes one of the last philosophical attempts to maintain the unity of reason in the face of the modern tendency to-

---

24. Wolfgang Amadeus Mozart, letter, n.d., cited in Edward Holmes, *The Life of Mozart* (1845; rpt. New York: Da Capo Press, 1979), pp. 317–18; this letter is cited by Heidegger in *The Principle of Reason*, p. 67.

ward the division of the world into discrete spheres. Leibniz sought to reconcile science and piety by integrating the atheism of particular mechanical explanations within a more profound view of the whole. As he himself writes: "I start out as a philosopher, but I end up a theologian. One of my great principles is that nothing is done without reason. It is a philosophical principle. Yet at root, it is nothing less than an acknowledgment of God's wisdom, although I do not speak of this at first."[25]

However, considered as a principle of *sufficient* reason, Leibniz's reflection is typically modern. It cannot think the goodness of existence as anything but a *value*. In so doing, it introduces the perspective of a subject who compares options and chooses the best one. The world's beauty is thus no longer immediately expressed by its order or the musical harmony of its parts. It is established only after passing through an order of values assigned by divine understanding to all the various possibilities available to it. By itself, the notion of *ratio* is vague and as apt to designate a mere relation of conformity as it is a strong logical relation between principle and consequence. Leibniz is modern in his belief that the good is more precisely defined as the *preferable*. At first glance, this modern view would seem to ruin every remaining possibility of linking existence with a beauty of the world as a whole. For if the entire world is beautiful, there is no way to *prefer* one part of it to another. Leibniz's genius reestablishes the world's goodness by displacing the decision by which only the best can be chosen. The *entire* world is declared good in the composition of all of its parts—the excellent as well as the imperfect and defective—by recourse to the model of a "rational" (in the modern sense) decision process to be applied to the infinite range of possibilities. Leibniz is modern in his belief that the act of saying "yes" to this world (as it exists) would be irrational, were it not determined by the fact that one and only one candidate had come to the fore to the exclusion of all the other possible worlds. It is not the notion of reason *tout court*, but the notion of *sufficient* reason, that leads Leibniz to seek the *harmonia*

---

25. In Eduard Bodemann, ed., *Die Leibniz-Handschriften der Königlichen öffentlichen Bibliothek zu Hannover* (Hildesheim: Georg Olms, 1966), p. 58.

mundi through the modern means offered by a "determining principle," a "divine mathematics," and a "metaphysical mechanism."[26]

The entire "question of existence" hinges on the way in which one is
attuned to what is. Attempts to characterize this "musical" disposition
are usually couched in a psychological or spiritual vocabulary: serenity, ennui, dread, joy, and so on. Alternatively, a whole series of technical "isms" may be used to describe the perspective that accompanies
each of these dispositions as either its expression or its motivation:
fatalism, pessimism, optimism, quietism. Lastly, one may avail oneself
of the austere terminology of philosophy in order to distinguish the
various forms of concord or discord between man and his world in
terms of the opposition between "yes" and "no," the acceptance or
refusal of "existence," that is, of what there is, such as it is. In a lecture
on contemporary French literature, Julien Gracq sets up an antithesis
between Paul Claudel's concept of literature and that of Jean-Paul
Sartre. According to Gracq, what is striking about Claudel is not his
Catholicism, but his "fundamental attitude toward the world," which
Gracq calls the "inclination to say 'yes' " [sentiment du oui]: "a daunt-
less, global yes, a *yes* that is almost voracious for the whole of creation."[27] Claudel undertakes no process of selection, Gracq notes, for
he accepts *everything*, the noble and the ignoble alike: "acceptance of
God, of creation, of the pope, of society, of France, of Pétain, of De
Gaulle, of money, of a well-remunerated career, of patriarchal pro-
geniture, of the great lineage that, in his words, he married in the
presence of a notary."[28] Sartre is exactly the opposite. His "attitude" is
that of a visceral *no*. *No* to nature, *no* to other people, *no* to the
existing society, *no* to every possible society ("he is the outcast, desig-
nated in advance, of every leftist political group, even those he attempted to found himself"), *no* to sexuality, *no* even to literary glory.
     Along with these two great fundamental attitudes—optimism and

---

26. Leibniz, "On the Radical Origination of Things," in *Philosophical Papers and
Letters*, pp. 487–88.

27. Julien Gracq, *Préférences* (Paris: José Corti, 1961), p. 92.

28. Ibid., p. 93.

pessimism, Claudel and Rosset's approbation and Sartre's refusal—
there is another "critical" attitude that one might call "rationalism":
yes if there is a good reason, *no* if not. And here we are attempting to
define another possible fundamental human attitude by means of an
analogy drawn from the epistemological dispute between rationalism
and empiricism.

For existentialist philosophers, all philosophical doctrines can be
traced back to "existential" attitudes. The "thesis concerning Being"
enunciated in the principle of reason ("Insofar as it exists, everything
that exists has a reason") must thus be regarded as a "worldview"—
that is, as if it were an assertion made by someone predisposed to
apprehend events in keeping with what we might call a "rationalist"
attitude.

Heidegger reverses this relationship. He accounts for the attitude
toward existence by means of the "thesis concerning Being." He thereby
removes from these fundamental attitudes (anguish, serenity, etc.) the
appearance of being subjective dispositions, states of mind, or merely
facts about human beings. Instead, he calls for an ontological formulation that would translate these attitudes toward existence into relations
between man and that which is *insofar as* it simply is (*ens qua ens*).

In order to subsume the "question of existence" within the "question of Being," Heidegger must assume that, whenever someone confronts something and recognizes that *there is something there*, in addition to the "ontic" relation (with a being that happens to be), an
"ontological" relation (with the Being of that being) is also established
between the recognizer and the recognized. The question of Being thus
arises everywhere, for it philosophically precedes every particular question. The fact that there are these various "fundamental attitudes"
only confirms, phenomenologically, that the question of Being is ubiq-
uitous. If one leaves aside Heidegger's speculation on the "history of
Being" (which must be considered as parasitical on his earlier premises), then the entire philosophical basis of his work amounts to the
idea that there is indeed this question of Being and that it is what
Heidegger says it is.[29] Moreover, Heidegger himself has said as much.

---

29. One might claim that when Heidegger takes it on himself to transcribe his version
of the history of metaphysics in terms of the "dispensations of Being," he pays a heavy

In the letter that serves as his preface to William J. Richardson's *Heidegger: Through Phenomenology to Thought*, Heidegger momentarily evokes what, to his mind, must seem an unlikely hypothesis: what if it were shown that the "question of Being" is "unjustified, superfluous, and impossible"?[30] Heidegger immediately dismisses the possibility, for he claims that it would amount to demonstrating (philosophically) that there are no philosophical questions, that every question is of an empirical or factual nature. This is why Heidegger's disciples deliberately claim that the "question of Being" is the "unavoidable" way of access to philosophy's present, and that everything in philosophy that does not revolve around this question in its Heideggerian formulation is little more than a fruitless distraction. In doing so, they do not seem disturbed by the fact that the philosophy of ancient Greece cannot be reduced to the line of thought that Heidegger has chosen to accentuate, nor do they seem to notice that modern philosophy is continuing without them.

Everyone agrees that metaphysics asks the "question of Being," that is, that it approaches its subject matter from the point of view of its Being. But these sorts of overly general statements lead nowhere, for they tell us nothing about how to actually practice metaphysical reduplication. In fact, Heidegger opted for a particular version of reduplication, one of several ways of understanding the *ens qua ens* with which metaphysics is concerned. And there is reason to believe that he chose the wrong version. In order to understand this point, we must be attentive to several distinctions related to what today might be called *philosophical grammar*, that is, an examination of

---

tribute to the intuitionist epistemology underlying every phenomenological undertaking. Indeed, it is paradoxical that the *appearance*, or "truth" (*alētheia*), of Being, which is supposed to take place every time that the question of Being is posed, is in fact *postulated* in order to satisfy Heidegger's preconceptions. For to demand that every understanding be founded in an appropriate eidetic intuition is an unwarranted presupposition. (On this point, see the chapters that Ernst Tugendhat devotes to Heidegger in his *Self-Consciousness and Self-Determination*, trans. Paul Stern [Cambridge, Mass.: MIT Press, 1986]). This is truly an amazing maneuver: to move from the "latent nonsense" of the notion of an intuition of Being to the "patent nonsense" of a history of Being, not in order to free oneself from illusion but to ensconce oneself in it all the more deeply.

30. Martin Heidegger, preface, in William J. Richardson, S.J., *Heidegger: Through Phenomenology to Thought* (The Hague: Martinus Nijhoff, 1963), p. xviii.

the most general concepts, analogical to the study of word functions in the construction of a sentence. This way of doing philosophy, first practiced by the great Greek metaphysicians, is rarely taken up by Heidegger, but enjoyed a revival in the work of thinkers like Russell and Wittgenstein.[31]

Aristotle provides an example of a metaphysical line of questioning (of "first philosophy," as he says). This example makes quite clear what is involved in the "question of Being" and, for Aristotle, serves to justify the addition of a distinct discipline—first philosophy—to the existing disciplines, each of which treats of a particular object: nature, mores, etcetera. Who other than a pure philosopher, he asks, will take it upon himself to find out whether Socrates is the same thing as Socrates-seated.[32] Put in the canonical form that itself comes out of Aristotle's work, the example boils down to something like this:

1. Biographical questions: What is true of Socrates? (examples: Where was he born? Who are his parents? What did he do? etc.)
2. Metaphysical questions: What is true of Socrates as a being? (the example provided: Are Socrates, who we assume is now seated, and Socrates-seated one and the same being?)

Admittedly, this type of metaphysical question—born of the disputes between Greek dialecticians and sophists—seems far removed from the inquiries into the justice of the world that make up the "question of existence." On the other hand, philosophical grammar, which asks, for example, how one might account for the difference between the proper noun "Socrates" and the adjective "seated," seems to be a direct descendant of this Aristotelian line of questioning.

---

31. In an interesting and tightly argued article, Gérard Guest attempts to reconcile Heidegger and Wittgenstein, but by giving primacy to hermeneutics (see "Interprétation et vérité," *Confrontations*, no. 17 [1987], pp. 7–24). He maintains that because philosophical grammar itself relies on various presuppositions, it is necessarily caught in a "hermeneutic circle." Following Wittgenstein, we may respond that interpretation cannot be *everywhere* if it hopes to be able to be *somewhere*: "Of course sometimes I do *interpret* signs, give signs an interpretation; but that does not happen every time I understand a sign." *Philosophical Grammar*, ed. Rush Rhees, trans. Anthony Kenny (Berkeley: University of California Press, 1974), p. 47.

32. Aristotle, *Metaphysics*, IV, 1004^{b}2.

Heidegger sees the piety of the world and European nihilism as responses to the "question of Being," because he is willing to grant a certain legitimacy to the project of a *general* metaphysics or ontology, the science of the *ens qua ens*. What he does not accept are the claims that such ontology is grounded in a reason that is itself well founded. It is a fact that sometimes we are dealing with Socrates as the subject of a biography, and sometimes with Socrates as a mere being. Thus, according to Heidegger, what it is to be a being is something that "appears" or "comes through" in every presentation of Socrates, whether physical or "intentional." Our relationships with Socrates, whether he is actually present before us or present before our mind's eye, are relationships with Socrates as a *being*, because they are relationships with he who *is* Socrates. There is thus a priority to be accorded to the relationship with Socrates as a being (*qua ens*), over and against all the relationships we may have with him in respect of any particular aspect under which he may be present to us. Moreover, we are willing to consider these particular facets only because they *are present*, or *could be present*, or *could have been present*.

Heidegger repeatedly articulated this doctrine of "preontological" comprehension in the course of his interpretation of Kant's work. He demonstrated that Kant's doctrine could be (and, according to him, *must* be) understood not as a general theory of knowledge, but as a foundation of the general metaphysics (or ontology) of the rationalist school, a foundation according to which the scope of metaphysics must be limited to what is given to us as phenomena. The first readers of Heidegger in France were themselves the students of Kantian professors. Though they were willing to contest their masters' reduction of first philosophy to epistemology, they naturally conceived ontology along the lines of the Kantian doctrine of the principles of objective judgment. One finds a good example of this classical doctrine in a work by Luc Ferry, one which nevertheless purports to criticize the Heideggerian position. Ferry reproaches Heidegger for having excluded values and "ethical vision" from his philosophy. But he starts out by conceding to Heidegger the validity of the project of a general metaphysics, unaware that this is precisely what prevents Heidegger from recognizing the autonomy of ethical questions.

> Unlike the sciences, philosophy does not study any particular object
> that really exists. To use the terms of Heideggerian phenomenology,
> it could be said that philosophy does not study any particular "be-
> ing," but instead questions itself "only" regarding the characteris-
> tics that are common to all "beings," common to every particular
> object *before* it has become an object of our concrete experi-
> ence.... For example, I can know—even before having seen a
> table, chair, or tree—that they all will be situated in space and time,
> that they will occupy a certain position in this space, that they will
> be to some extent identical with themselves... that they will
> have... a reason for existence or, if you like, a cause, etcetera.[33]

This account (which Ferry himself admits is oversimplified and sche-
matic) provides a good illustration of how metaphysical reduplication
operates among the partisans of general metaphysics. The passage
from the "ontic" point of view to the "ontological" one can be formulated as follows:

1. *Without reduplication*, we obtain in response to our questions regarding the object Socrates (Who is Socrates? What is Socrates?) a
   biographical description made up of a set of particular characteristics (like his status within society, his career, etc.), a description that
   is only made determinate by our experience.
2. *With ontological reduplication*, we are offered an "ontological"
   description of Socrates, a description of Socrates not as a particular
   person, or even as an example of a particular species, but as a *being*:
   the ontological description does not provide us with Socrates' *par-
   ticulars* (which are unique because they are contingent) but with the
   characteristics that Socrates possesses *qua ens*, as a being, and that
   are thus shared by *every* being.

The point made by these partisans is that there are two possible
descriptions of any object: it can be described either as the particular
object that it is, or as an object exhibiting the fundamental properties
(the "categories") of every object in general, of the object "X" in

---

33. Luc Ferry, *Philosophie politique* (Paris: Presses Universitaires de France, 1984),
II, 19. An English translation of this volume has recently been published: Luc Ferry, *The
System of Philosophies of History,* trans. Franklin Philip (Chicago: University of Chi-
cago Press, 1992).

general. And, as Heidegger points out, the same metaphysical structure underlies both rationalist ontology and the epistemology of critical philosophy, in virtue of these equivalences:

ens (ontology) = object (epistemology)
entitas (ontology) = objectivity (epistemology)
ontologia = transcendental philosophy (epistemology)

One might well find Aristotle's way of proceeding preferable to this modern one. If we think of ourselves as more Aristotelian than Suarezian or Wolffian, then we will avoid overly general declarations about the object *as* object, in order to return to the sources of the whole question: for example, "Is Socrates the same as Socrates-seated?" This is a genuinely metaphysical question, one that bears on what Socrates is as a being. One might respond with the following line of reasoning: if Socrates is the same thing as Socrates-seated (the example assumes that Socrates is in a seated position in front of us), then Socrates-standing (the example assumes that Socrates was standing and has just sat down) is not the same being as Socrates-seated. According to this (metaphysical) hypothesis, our language must be reformed. There are two ways of doing this: we may either adopt an ontology of ephemeral individuals, or one of individuals as processes. If we adopt the first ontology, then when we speak of Socrates, first standing and then sitting, we are fooled by our language: what we call "Socrates" is not one, single individual but a series of ephemeral individuals that rapidly succeed one another. If, on the other hand, we adopt the second ontology, then when we speak of Socrates, we are not referring to an inalterable individual, but to everything that would be contained in a complete and truthful biography of Socrates. By this view, Socrates is really an entire process that spans the time between his birth and his death; thus at any given moment, we will never confront the individual called Socrates, but only a temporal "slice" of the individual/ process Socrates who is a spatio-temporal being. Consequently, it is not Socrates who is seated, but Socrates-at-the-present-moment, one part or slice of Socrates.

Aristotle's solution is to invent the categories. He starts out by refusing to identify Socrates and Socrates-seated. Socrates is a being, but Socrates-seated is the "accidental" encounter of *two* beings: a human being and a position of the body. What is Socrates as a being? He is not an object in general but a man, namely, the man whose humanity is that of Socrates. What is Socrates-seated as a being? He is, once again, a man who is in a sitting position. What can we say about "who-is-in-a-sitting-position" as a being? It is a position that *is* only if there happens (by "accident") to be someone to assume it.

A clearer formulation of this Aristotelian analysis results if we observe one of the tenets of Fregean analytic philosophy, according to which we should not ask the general question "What is Socrates?" (nor "What is man?") but rather a question concerning identity: "With what is Socrates identical and in what measure?" (Or, "What is it for an individual to be *the same man* as himself?") One then obtains the following solutions to the paradox of change (in this example, the change consists in sitting down):

1. Socrates (whatever his position) is *the same man* as Socrates-seated.
2. The relative expression "who is seated" refers to *the same sitting position*, if it is said more than once of the same body and this body is indeed each time in this sitting position.

Here ontology does not take the form of a general metaphysics. There is no ontological description of the *ens in genere*, no properties that are ascribed to all beings, for beings are too heterogeneous. The "categories" are no longer treated as the properties of every object or as the conditions of possibility of objectivity. Rather, they are the predicamental lines by which we recognize that something is there: they are substances, places, times, actions, passions, structures and relations, etcetera. After all, what could a substance (Socrates) and an action (the movement of sitting down) possibly have in common? The most one can expect are *relations* between these things (there is only a movement of sitting down if there is a body to be so moved, etc.).

But the partisans of general metaphysics have never really accepted the diversity of the meanings of "Being" (of the word "Being"). They persist in trying to find the kernel of "transcendental" meaning that would be at the origin of all the various uses of the ontological vocabulary. They claim, for example, that all beings (substances and accidents) have presence, *energeia*, actuality, and effectivity in common.

From this they conclude that there is a single meaning of "Being." And since this single meaning has been variously determined in the course of the history of philosophy, there must be several significations (each one univocal) of "Being," each of which gives rise to a different "epoch of Being." But this defense of metaphysics is not as clear as Heidegger's disciples think it is. For each time one makes an attempt to say something more about *presence*, one is led back to one of the specific ontological regions that will be distinguished by a general ontology. In fact, presence as such is always conceived according to the paradigm provided by a particular *type* of presence, whether it be the material presence of an inert body, the active presence of a living being, or the ideal presence of a geometrical figure. And if this is the case, then perhaps there really is neither a "meaning of Being" nor any possible use of the phrase "there is" [*il y a*] that is *independent* of what, in each case, takes on the appropriate form of Being.

In any case, this is Aristotle's opinion. I need not offer any further defense of this view. It suffices that it exist for my purposes, for it follows from this that one can ask a "question of Being" that has nothing to do with the "question of existence." In *De anima* Aristotle writes that "in the case of living things, their being is to live" ($415^{b}13$). The medieval scholastics derived from this a multipurpose adage: "Vivere viventibus est esse." If we take this idea seriously, it follows that there is no need to provide two descriptions of the living thing named Socrates, one presenting him as a particular man and another as a transcendental object. This is not to say that we should make no distinction between a biographical description and a metaphysical characterization, for that would amount to the sort of inept positivism that Heidegger's disciples tell us is unavoidable if we do not accept the Heideggerian version of the "question of Being." On the contrary, the distinction persists in the following way: Socrates' biography does not tell us that Socrates is a man, for it is only comprehensible as the narrative of Socrates' life if we *already* know what sort of being Socrates is; on the other hand, this biography does tell us what Socrates *happened* to be, his adventures, his transformations, what happened to him, what he stopped being (without, however, ceasing to be Socrates—the particular human being—until the day of his death). As for the metaphysical determination, it tells us what no biography can because every biography presupposes it: namely, what type of being Socrates is.

This entire discussion can be summarized as follows:

1. For the partisan of general metaphysics, the table, the chair, and the tree (to use Ferry's example) are ontologically the same thing; as beings they have the same features (those of objectivity or of "being-an-object").
2. For the Aristotelian way of asking the "question of Being," the table, the chair, and the tree are ontologically distinct from one another: the tree is a living substance while the table and the chair are not substances but physical structures.

Their mode of Being or presence is therefore different. There is thus no need to look for some always-identical *relation to Being* in the fact that we have an ontological understanding of trees as beings or of furnishings as beings. According to this second version of the "question of Being," there is no need to seek, underlying all our particular relations with the things that occupy us, *another* relation with the Being of these things, a relation that would stem from the mere fact that these things are beings, that for us they constitute what is. Indeed, the *ens in genere*, the object considered indifferently in its object-hood, cannot be described in any way that is not contentless. But if general ontology is necessarily vacuous, then the attempt to dissolve the "question of existence" within the "question of Being" is doomed to failure. The "question of existence" preserves its autonomy and its philosophical legitimacy outside metaphysical distinctions. The "question of Being" always bears on the specific form of Being that we recognize a given being as having. The "question of existence" is our response to the fact that life is what it is, that the things affecting us are what they are and not otherwise. Thus the two questions do not overlap: each of them has its own weight. The tendency to conflate the two may well result from the ambiguity of the expression "the meaning of Being," that is sometimes taken to be equivalent to "the meaning of the word 'is' in a given sentence," and sometimes treated as meaning "the attitude that makes us say 'yes' or 'no' to the world taken as a whole, without allowing us to choose."

Of course sometimes the "question of existence" disguises itself as the "question of Being." Once the various forms of Being have been distinguished—usually by dividing beings into the inert, the living, and the spiritual or conceptual—philosophers attempt to organize them. They construct "great chains of Being," scales establishing degrees of Being. Today these ontological hierarchies are suspect, for we are no longer willing to adopt a hierarchical vision of things, whereas this way of thinking seemed entirely natural for thinkers operating within a traditional culture. When *we* attempt to conceive of a system or world, we prefer to do so using the notion of *solidarity* (or reciprocity) rather than that of *subordination*. For us, categories of dignity can only be categories of value and thus must be viewed as "subjective." We can understand it when a farmer establishes rankings within his world: the animals in the courtyard, the people in the house, the masters in the nicest bedroom. But we also know that this is only the farmer's view, one not necessarily shared by the dogs or the chickens. In other words, we no longer see the hierarchy as ontological: one only adopts a particular hierarchy among other possible hierarchies after having adopted a point of view that is only one among many such possible points of view. I find it difficult to deny that the difference between our egalitarian view of things and the traditional hierarchical view is not a matter of pure ontology but one of *culture*. Philosophism acts as though Western culture were *contained within* Western metaphysics. But the reverse formulation is more accurate: the various Western metaphysics *grew out of* Western culture.

Incontestably, it is always possible to lay bare the (regional) ontology implicit in a theory, project, or attitude. If only Heideggerian philosophy were able to limit the scope of its legitimate demand for an ontological clarification of a given epoch's conceptions, it would be on solid ground, a ground that it would share—and this is a major inconvenience for *intensified* thought—with *other* philosophies. Indeed, the inquiry into the metaphysics of modern science or the metaphysics of the revolutionary project is a necessary undertaking. But these inquiries would seem to necessitate a more *applied* approach than that of the Heideggerians: no longer the metaphysics of science in general, as if there were necessarily only one, but the metaphysics of a particular science and its particular interpretations; no longer the metaphysics of

Revolution, but the metaphysics of the collective entities of Jacobinism, Fabian socialism, Leninism, and so on.

In all these metaphysical inquiries, it is difficult to see how one could
dispense with a kind of "fieldwork," examining the ontological concepts *at work* and as they actually function. The idea that philosophical questions should never be given a particular form or be posed from
within a specific discipline seems to me particularly inappropriate.
Here Heidegger may well have embraced the most debatable of rationalist prejudices: that philosophical disciplines are not really autonomous; that the traditional division of philosophical questions (into the
logical, the physical, the ethical, etc.) are without foundation; that
because, as rationalists believe, the principles of each of these orders
can be derived from the universal principles of reason, all of them are
without principles of their own.

Critics of Western metaphysics never tire of denouncing the nihilis-
tic act of will that, according to them, has been disguised as a "rational" endeavor: the search for foundations and reasons. But their
claims leave one with an ambiguous impression. For at the same time
that they accuse metaphysics of not *letting beings be*, they themselves
seem to get carried away in another sort of metaphysical frenzy
wherein they refuse to let philosophical research be what *it* is: essays,
propositions, and ideas presented for our consideration; arguments
that will always need to be scrutinized.

The hermeneutical version of the phenomenology of Being ends up
becoming almost indistinguishable from the most extreme sort of *ideology critique*. What is unacceptable about the ideological destruction of
ideas is that there is no way to defend against it. If "everything is
political," then anything you might say will fall into one of two classes
of utterances: on the one hand, your infrequent political declarations
where you lay down your mask, as it were; on the other, all your other
statements in which you do nothing more than *disguise* your political
position as science, art, love, joy, and the like. Similarly, if "everything is
desire," all discourse is then divided into explicit demands where desire
is out in the open, and libidinal expressions that have been disguised as
observations, questions, answers, speculations, etcetera. This is an example of the extreme strategy that holds that one and only one thing is
necessary. If the only justifiable concern is one's own salvation, every-

thing else is mere diversion. This idea is a profound one, if it leads me to hole up in my room and meditate. But to transpose it into worldly affairs is to invite disaster. The politics of this view is fanaticism. And the corresponding psychology is a maniacal interpretation.

Here we might hazard a hypothesis regarding Heidegger's success among French philosophers, a success that is difficult to attribute to a simple interest in logical and metaphysical questions. These questions are admittedly no longer French philosophy's forte. Nor has it been observed that the enormous recognition accorded to Heidegger's philosophy has in any way led the public to delve into the arduous texts of Western metaphysics. Heidegger may have inspired a few hardy souls to read Plato's *Parmenides* or the Scholastic *Summae*, but one suspects that these people would have read those works regardless, and deep down they may even regret having to accuse them of nihilism. But Heideggerian argumentation serves another purpose. Heidegger provides the philosopher with a means of *one-upmanship* in the confrontation among the various contemporary forms of demystification. To say that "the Totality is metaphysical" is to adopt a position so radical that it easily outstrips previous demystifications. The unmasking of philosophy has long been urged by various groups that by turns have held either that philosophy expresses only the views of a particular social class, or that it is the manifestation of paranoid desire, or that it is lacking in vital energy. For those whose trade is the teaching of philosophy, such claims are understandably distressing. These people were therefore delighted to find in the hermeneutics of the "dispensations of Being" a way of thinking that completely liberates the philosophical tradition from its role in this world (i.e., its *applications*), at the same time that it provides the reader with the means for exposing what remains *unthought* in the positions of its adversaries. One cannot defend oneself against this strategy: all opposing discourse is criticized on the basis of what is implicit in the most general terms of its vocabulary—that is, in those words that every discourse inevitably uses, words like "nature," "object," "existence," "form," "force," "self," etcetera. The moment the enemy of philosophy begins to reduce metaphysics to a political or sexual ideology, he has already lost the battle, for he must necessarily use some of the words that make up the vocabulary of Western metaphysics.

Nevertheless, this invincible strategy exacts a price that the philoso-pher might not be willing to pay. For in order to rescue philosophy from the attacks of ideology critique, he must henceforth forgo any use of the metaphysical vocabulary other than within quotation marks or "under erasure." He must cease doing the very thing that seemed most valuable to him when he became a philosopher: he must cease doing philosophy.

The reader may be surprised that in a chapter devoted to the Hei-deggerian way of thinking about the epoch, I have yet to say a word about what many think is the real issue: What is the relationship between Heidegger the doctor of metaphysics and Heidegger the Hit-lerian rector? In 1988 the "Heidegger Affair" was on the front pages of all the French newspapers. It was even discussed in "illustrated magazines." This would certainly seem to be a good example of a philosopher whose judgments regarding the current events of his own time have become part of the current events of ours.

My excuse is that Heidegger seems to me to have never made a philosophical judgment that *also* bore on the events of his time. Of course Heidegger's thought has the pretention to being a meditation on the "metaphysics of the modern age." I believe I have shown here that the very notion of a "metaphysics of the age" is incoherent and that this incoherence is rooted in the inflection given to the "question of Being" itself. I think it admirable that many of Heidegger's readers have found, within the "question of Being," passages that lead, accord-ing to some, to the worst political aberrations (those of Heidegger the rector) and, according to others, to a greater lucidity regarding the traps set by the age (the lucidity Heidegger would have demonstrated, had he chosen to remain the doctor of metaphysics, faithful to his original "questioning"). It is true that Heidegger interprets the "ques-tion of Being" in an extremely original way, calling on it to satisfy two requirements: Being must be *univocal* (without becoming merely con-ceptual or generic), and it must be *phenomenologically* accessible (without being reduced to a lived, vital, or "existential" experience). This line of metaphysical questioning not only seems to me to lead to a philosophical impasse, it also seems devoid of any *political cast* what-soever. It may well be that those readers who claim to have no difficulty making the transition from Heideggerian metaphysics to politics are really only too happy to find themselves on more familiar ground.

But what about the "political texts" where Heidegger combines Nazi jargon with the technical terminology of *Sein und Zeit*? These distressing declarations do indeed contain a number of sentences that are undeniably political. This one, for example: "*Heil Hitler!*" Others are typically metaphysical. What is missing is any kind of link between the two. Thus in an appeal for a *yes* vote in the plebiscite of November 12, 1933, Heidegger declares that only this vote can satisfy the "the essential law of human *Dasein*" by which each people is responsible for itself. Each *Dasein*, he writes, seeks to "preserve and save its own essence."[34] We should have no difficulty recognizing in this the old maxims according to which "Bonum convertitur cum ente," or "Est aliquid bonum, inquantum est ens." Everything that is, is good insofar as it is and thus exists in accordance with the "law" that "commands" it to persevere in its Being and to safeguard its proper form of Being. This statement about human *Dasein* is a metaphysical one. What is lacking in this text, as in the others, is any indication of what sort of political decision might be made on the basis of such a "law." I am not claiming here that Heidegger drew the wrong conclusions from a sound philosophy, nor that he carried a contemptible philosophy to its logical conclusions. Rather, what is striking is the absence of a conclusion in these texts, their construction which is—to use the adjective with which Heidegger attacks the logic of propositions—"paratactic." It is difficult to see how one could conclude *anything* about the way one should vote at a plebiscite on the basis of the metaphysical axiom according to which "what is good for a people is to be." Why is the preservation of the German people to be sought in the surrender to Hitler rather than in resistance to him? This is precisely the sort of question that requires a political judgment. Perhaps because Heidegger thought that we could encounter Being itself, he did not take into account the necessity of what used to be called "intermediary axioms," axioms without which one cannot move from first principles which are incontestable but formal, to their judicious application.

---

34. This text appears in the collection of "political texts" translated into English by William S. Lewis and published in *New German Critique*, no. 45 (1988), p. 105.

= 6 =

The Demystification of the World

> Myths overlap or oppose one another, depending on
> one's point of view: my totem is quite large, yours is
> rather small.
>
> Mauss, *Manuel d'ethnographie*[1]

Critical Theory and the deconstruction of the epochal metaphysics of
the West share a philosophistic postulate: *In every way, modernity
means rationality*. I call this postulate philosophistic because it tends
to turn the sequence of great axioms, or first principles, into the vari-
able of which all other historical mutations of culture are the functions. In turn, the succession of these axioms, or the philosophical
tradition, is seen to have as its law the search for "coherent discourse."
According to this legend, the entire history of the West continually
repeats on a grander and grander scale the first scene described in any
course on the history of ancient philosophy: *myth* gives way to *reason*.
What Max Weber called the "disenchantment" of the world consists
in this extension of the critical practice of philosophers to all aspects of
existence.

Often philosophers feel obligated to maintain this view of their task.
According to them, if philosophy is anything at all, it is an attempt to
think radically. Thus if I am a philosopher, I am obliged to believe that
the philosopher's act of thinking immediately liberates him from age-
old prejudices. Rationality should *then* spread to public opinion and
develop into a generalized Enlightenment. It is the philosopher's job to

---

1. Marcel Mauss, *Manuel d'ethnographie*, 2nd ed. (Paris: Payot, 1967), p. 250.

work toward the construction of a rational civilization, and he cannot escape this without falling into contradiction.

Yet there are profound difficulties with using the concept of rationality in order to describe our culture as rational or rationalized. This fact is obvious to those historians seeking to demonstrate the greatness of "dark" ages, just as it is to anthropologists seeking to understand peoples whose ways of thinking are quite different from our own. But insufficient attention is given to the fact that philosophers, too, should be more careful when speaking about rationality.[2] Perhaps we need to reconsider the task of the philosopher.

A philosopher's job usually involves examining propositions, not in order to subject them to experimental verification or some sort of calculation, but in order to understand them and, perhaps, to accept or reject them for reasons that are purely philosophical. The philosopher's vocation thus requires him to distinguish the *meaning* of a proposition from its *truth*. This distinction is the gateway to the logical point of view. For every true proposition, there must be a corresponding false proposition—its negation. But this false proposition cannot be such unless it has meaning. Not only must it be meaningful, but its meaning must be as clear as that of the corresponding true proposition, for it offers the same conceptual content only subject to negation. If, therefore, we consider rationality in a philosophical manner—as the correct construction of discourse—we necessarily suppose that the true proposition and the corresponding false proposition considered in themselves are equally rational.

Thus the proposition "witches do not exist" cannot be true unless the proposition "witches do exist" is false. Now the proposition "witches do exist" cannot be false if it is meaningless. And for it to have the meaning required for it to be declared false, it must be minimally rational. If the very idea that witches *may* exist is held to be "irrational," then it is just as "irrational" to claim that witches do not exist, for in such a case one no longer knows what one is talking about—what claim about the *natura rerum* is to be accepted or rejected.

---

2. In this regard see Alasdair MacIntyre, "Rationality and the Explanation of Action," in his *Against the Self-Images of the Age* (London: Duckworth, 1971), pp. 244–59.

On the other hand, it truly is irrational to believe in witches, while subscribing with equal or greater conviction to dogmas that exclude any possibility of witchcraft. Notice, however, that it is just as irrational *not to believe* in the possibility of witchcraft, if one also subscribes to a general view of things by which witchcraft must at least be possible. In other words, one cannot determine that a given belief is irrational, unless one is also familiar with the believer's *other* beliefs. But what do we mean by "a person's beliefs"? How are we to know what someone believes? In reality, an individual's beliefs do not take the form of an immense personal credo: it is not as though one could list all the beliefs that make up one's dogma and fix its limits with exactitude. Nor is it possible to exteriorize the entirety of one's beliefs by checking the appropriate boxes on some kind of giant questionnaire ("Do you believe that Julius Caesar existed?" "Do you believe there are tigers in South America?", etc.). These questions seem to us wrongheaded. To speak of a *set* of beliefs only makes sense if one considers them *outside* of their relation to the subject of belief, the believer. Instead, they should be considered in relation to a totality above and beyond individuals: an epoch or a culture. Unless we have serious reasons to dissent, we generally believe what those around us believe. Thus an individual who is asked about the *totality* of his beliefs is usually overwhelmed, unless of course he happens to have an encyclopedia on hand to which he might refer us. For an encyclopedia offers a good representation of the collection of beliefs that each of us holds to be true without, for all that, being shocked if most of the articles are subject to correction from time to time.

A philosophy of belief must accordingly be "holistic" rather than "atomistic." We should then attach the following qualification to the use of the concept of rationality: in order for a given example of thought—whether in the form of a representation (a predication), a discourse (a proposition), an association of ideas (an inference), or an attitude (belief, hope, etc.)—to be qualified as rational or irrational, one must be able to indicate the *set* of thoughts to which it belongs as an element. Rationality and irrationality are only at issue where there is a construction whose parts must be compatible with one another. As a result, the irrationality of someone's opinions only appears in the context of other opinions—also held by the person in question—that are incompatible with the opinions qualified as irrational. When opinions are incompatible in this way, how does one then go about ascribing irrationality to one of them? By looking at those that can be sacrificed while taking as given those that one is not prepared to modify. Whenever a contradiction is discovered between an "archaic" belief and an "enlightened" worldview, it is irrational to preserve the archaic opinion, but this is true only if one refuses to revise the enlightened opinions in a way that would remove the contradiction.

It follows that no culture, whether "primitive" or "advanced," is irrational. Nor are all cultures rational. Rather, the notion of rationality is simply inapplicable so long as we are unable to establish a contrast between a particular body of opinions (that fragment of the whole that is subject to revision) and a framework of certitudes. Is it irrational to believe in witches? This question does not mean quite the same thing as another question with which it is often confused: Do witches exist? Though I will not hesitate to answer that there are no witches, if I am then asked why, I will only be able to provide the reasons that lead us to this conclusion today. The villager who believes in witches may well be wrong (because there are no witches), but this does not necessarily mean that his belief is irrational. This contrast, between the opinion whose rationality is in question and the background beliefs that form the basis for our judging it, can only be established within a given culture.

Those who say that our own civilization is an expression of "modern reason," or that it is the result of a process of rationalization, have thus fallen prey to a powerful misconception. We imagine someone (an individual subject) to whom various *options* have been presented: he might prefer to "believe in science" or, alternatively, he might opt to "believe in myth." If he chooses science, we call him rational. This representation of things rests on a misunderstanding. In order to make a choice that is motivated, he must have at his disposal not only logical criteria (noncontradiction, etc.), but also *paradigms* illustrating what counts as a good explanation, a good analysis, a good decision, a good justification, and so on. Culture is what provides these paradigms as part of the education and upbringing of newcomers. It follows that a radical choice among cultural possibilities is illusory.

I have insisted on this point because I feel it is important to recognize that we have *philosophical reasons* for wanting to escape the alternative between "reason" and "myth." Merely by being philosophers, we are on the side of "reason." But what do we know about the other side? How do we know that on the other side lurks our adversary, namely, myth? How do we know that there is only one "other side" opposed to our own? Why should there be, as is often supposed, an Other of Reason that, since the Enlightenment, has been called Myth, the heir of Fable? In this context, the concept of myth is always more or less that of its literary reconstruction. Myth is a founding narrative, a tale about origins. An opposition has accordingly been set up between the un-reasoned, narrative, imagistic discourse of myth and the reasoned—whether deductive or factual—univocal discourse of science. But even if we remain within the terms of literary theory, why should we neglect the fact that there is a *variety* of literary forms? Why should myth—and not, say, proverb, legend, enigma, *exemplum,* etcetera—be singled out as *the* Other of the discourse regulated by critical reason?[3] Here again we encounter all the deficiencies of logical Manichaeism. If we hope to continue to define philosophy as an exercise in radical thought, we will have to find another way of practicing it. We will have to find a way out of the false alternative between positivism and transcendental thought, and we will have to do this for the simple reason that this opposition assumes that philosophical discussion goes on someplace other than in this world. Such a conception is not only chimerical, it is philosophically incoherent. As a result, the entire problem posed by the "disenchant-ment" and "modernization" of the world must be taken up anew from this perspective. In these last two chapters I hope to sketch out this indispensable conceptual revision.

We may begin with the debate regarding the "postmodern." The very success of this adjective—an adjective whose opacity is univer-sally acknowledged—indicates a disturbance of opinion. We had grown accustomed to seeing all human endeavors—whether technical innovations, stylistic inventions, or theoretical breakthroughs—as be-ing cumulative in the same way that sports records are cumulative:

---

3. André Jolles has proposed drawing distinctions among legends, sagas, myths, riddles, locutions, cases, memorabilia, tales, and witticisms. See his *Einfache Formen* (Tübingen: M. Niemeyer, 1958).

each success temporarily raises a hero to the limit of human capabilities. The old record holder must give up his title and take his place among the other former greats in the Hall of Fame. To talk about the postmodern is to admit that things can no longer be represented in this way. What is new today in no way surpasses the new things of yesterday: it does not go farther, higher, faster, stronger, or even in the same direction. It is nevertheless new, for the modern is henceforth marked as what was done *earlier*.

In all of this, it is not the word "postmodern" that is most important. If people cease to feel that this term is applicable, others will certainly be found. More important, this idea that we are at a point, as it were, *after* progress and at the end of history has already been expressed several times through various other words. Each of these words indicates that we are no longer entirely within the age of the *modern project*. We are not part of the generation of *strong men* (Baudelaire) who realized this project through the work of Revolution. We are rather their children and grandchildren. We thus not only receive their inheritance as it stands, but must also pay off the outstanding debts. The Revolution gave birth to a mindset that was neither that of the defunct ancien régime nor that of revolutionary grandeur. As indicative of a disquiet underlying the entire century, this mindset was known as romanticism, Wagnerism, symbolism, decadence, and so on. But it could also give rise to bursts of energy called Saint-Simonism, positivism, Baudelairean *modernity*, socialism (in the original sense of the word), etcetera. How are we to understand this cyclothymic[4] oscillation, these fits of *spleen*, these futuristic awakenings?

Perhaps the best bet is the following observation: for most people, the word "modern" above all suggests an obligation—often traumatic—to modernize *oneself*. It constitutes an obligation to modernize one's technologies, one's mores, and one's way of thinking, and all this as a way of merely surviving. But it is not simply a question of material survival in a universe ruled by relations of force: this kind of Darwinism might justify the modernization of armaments, but not the sorts of crises of conscience or mental distress that are at issue here. For one must above

---

4. Translator's note: "Cyclothymic" is a term coined by the psychiatrist Emile Kraepelin to describe the alternation between states of agitation and depression.

all survive *morally*, through the preservation of one's self-esteem. In other words, the obligation to modernize oneself is an obligation to demonstrate that one is the equal not only of the more modern foreign *power* that one confronts, but especially of its alien *spirit*. It is this moral component of the process of modernization that is most exacting. If it were merely a matter of borrowing recipes and procedures, one would only need to worry about financing the modernization of equipment. What is difficult is the modernization of minds. To be able to accept modern ideas instead of disgustedly rejecting them as inhuman, lacking in piety, or preposterous, a complex state of mind is required. In order to succeed in imitating one's more prestigious foreign neighbors, it suffices to envy them. But in order to recognize the *value* of the modern, the nobility of modern ideals, one must discover the moral resources of one's own tradition. Anyone who is ashamed of the customs of his own country is in fact incapable of being profoundly stirred by modern ideas. The psychological structure of someone undergoing the process of modernization is thus exceedingly complex. He must experience a certain fascination with the ideas in vogue elsewhere (in London, in Paris, in the United States), for without this he will never come to criticize the ideas of his parents, neighbors, and teachers. But at the same time he must also reestablish the superiority of the ideas of his own country, or he runs the risk of wallowing in inconsistency or nihilism. This psychological structure can be found among more than one of the heroes of postmodernism: the German romantic, for example, who is obsessed with both the idea of the absolute Freedom of the Self and that of the absence of divine presence; or the characters of Dostoyevski who move without warning between support for Western ideas and the most fanatical Pan-Slavic convictions.

In short, as I understand it here, and following Louis Dumont,[5] the postmodern can be understood as an element opposed to the modern in a process that contains them both: the process of the modernization of the world. As long as we are referring to modern ideas, we can limit our discussion to a single national tradition, or even to a single national

---

5. See Louis Dumont, "Identités collectives et idéologie universaliste: leur interaction de fait," *Critique*, no. 456 (1985); and his "Are Cultures Living Beings?: German Identity in Interaction," *Man*, n.s., no. 21 (1986).

capital. On the other hand, to speak of a process of modernization is to introduce the perspective of an interaction of national cultures. The real inventors of modern ideas have no intention of modernizing. They are reformers and revolutionaries who seek to bring things back to an initial state in which they should have been conserved. On the other hand, if one is eager to modernize things, it is only because one has a more modern neighbor to imitate. Far from being an expression of an autonomous reason discovering that it must be grounded upon itself, modernization is what anthropologists call a "process of acculturation." Whenever a modern culture and a traditional culture come into contact, the modern one provokes the other into reestablishing its collective identity through the invention of more or less felicitous syntheses between elements of the modern culture and elements of its own.

For Jean-François Lyotard, the elaboration of the notion of the postmodern begins as a reconsideration of what the critical theory of the Frankfurt School referred to as the *Dialectic of Enlightenment.*[6] This elaboration therefore shares the deficiencies of every theory based on the logical Manichaeism of reason and its Other. Indeed, the dialectic of Enlightenment takes place between two concepts: reason and myth. There is a dialectic if, in its effects—its *accomplishments*—reason is in the end indistinguishable from myth. For Lyotard, the modern moment is that of the ruin of the founding narratives around which traditional cultures were organized. Modern reason is thus a sort of antifable. But today we have come to realize that reason itself derived its power from another sort of fable: the philosophies of history. Ancient myths were directed toward the origin: they were therefore only capable of founding different *particular* communities. The origin they described was always that of *our* community, of *us*, the true people, as opposed to *them*, those whose way of life is hopelessly misguided. Critical reason replaces these particular narratives with universal ideals. These ideals come to us in the form of great eschatological narra-

---

6. Jean-François Lyotard, *The Postmodern Condition*, trans. Geoff Bennington and Brian Massumi (Minneapolis: University of Minnesota Press, 1984). Theodor W. Adorno and Max Horkheimer, *Dialectic of Enlightenment*, trans. John Cumming (New York: Seabury, 1972).

tives announcing the advent of a new, emancipated man who will be reconciled with himself. By destroying our confidence in narrative as a source of authority, critical modernity ends up depriving modern endeavors of the legitimacy such narratives provided. This is the moment of "delegitimation" and the "postmodern." *Modern man* believed that there was a sense and direction to history. He was thus able to take sides on issues, support various causes, and commit himself to political organizations. *Postmodern man* is the same modern man after his critical spirit has overcome the last remnants of credulity: he no longer believes in the "great narratives" of liberalism or Marxism. For postmodern man, modern endeavors go on *without us*, for they exclude any sort of legitimation in terms of moral progress, the emancipation of the human race, or the construction of a promising future. Science and technology "develop" on their own and have no other goal than an increase in efficiency, ever-greater "performance" and rapidity, etcetera. Here again there is a dialectical coincidence of rationality and absurdity.

But Lyotard extends his analysis. Through the notion of the *differend*[7] he offers a perspective by which to escape the impasses of a pure dialectic of Enlightenment. It seems to me that Lyotard provides a useful reframing of the question by refusing to stop with the Enlightenment, in order to turn his attention to the profound ambiguity of the French Revolution. Lyotard maintains that in 1789 a (nondialectical) tension was introduced into our history when a particular community presumed to speak for humanity as a whole. The Preamble to the Declaration of the Rights of Man and Citizen of 1789 reads: "The representatives of the French people, organized in National Assem-

---

7. Translator's note: The English translator of Lyotard's *Le différend* has chosen to translate the word with the English neologism "differend." I follow this usage here. For though the term différend is an everyday French word meaning "dispute," "disagreement," or "conflict," Lyotard uses it in the following technical sense: "A case of differend between two parties takes place when the 'regulation' of the conflict that opposes them is done in the idiom of one of the parties, while the wrong suffered by the other is not signified in that idiom." Jean-François Lyotard, *The Differend*, trans. Georges Van Den Abbeele (Minneapolis: University of Minnesota Press, 1988), p. 9; see also the glossary on pp. 193–95.

bly . . . have resolved to set forth in a solemn declaration the natural, inalienable, and sacred rights of man."[8] The signatory of this declaration is not humanity as a whole, nor is it some would-be universal spiritual authority. Rather, it is the National Assembly of the representatives of the French people. There is thus a dangerous ambiguity in the inaugural act of the *legitimate* history of France: a single word from the political lexicon, the word "people," is used to refer both to a particular, historical collective replete with its own stock of legends that tell of great deeds, heroes, and heroines, and at the same time, to the temporary representatives of humanity's most profound interests. Thus it is that the French political tradition comes to be divided between its de jure universalism and its de facto particularism. This tension reemerges in the appeal made by these representatives of the people to the higher authority of the Supreme Being. But why should the Supreme Being empower a particular nation? Suddenly the altruistic politics of the French Revolution fall into the legendary schema of the "gesta Dei per Francos."

This results in what Lyotard calls a *differend*, a disagreement between claims voiced in heterogeneous idioms (idioms that are "incommensurable" in Thomas Kuhn's sense of the word), a disagreement that is in some ways insurmountable. Seen from France, revolutionary politics is by definition one of Freedom for all human beings. Wherever French troops advance, they liberate people from oppression by despots. This is, for example, the view of Stendhal in *La chartreuse de Parme*: the fresh, gay, inspirited French republicans, who dazzle the young maidens of Milan and fire the imagination of the young liberals, encounter opposition only among old fogies. But, seen from abroad, the revolutionary politics of France is nothing more than the power politics of an impassioned people. Viewed from France, the Declaration calls only for moral judgment. And how could such judgment be anything but approving, when confronted with such lofty principles? Kant put it well: as long as the people of Europe see the Revolution as a spectacle without consequences for them, it cannot but elicit their

---

8. Cited in Lyotard, *The Differend*, p. 145.

enthusiasm. But viewed from the perspective of experienced ministers of state abroad, the Declaration is a political act requiring a political reaction, a harbinger of imminent annexations, propaganda campaigns, and attempts at subversion.

The *differend* can thus be expressed as follows: "After 1789, international wars are also civil wars."[9] Thus it is that the two world wars that tore Europe apart have been subject to two standards and two irreconcilable rhetorics. For the partisans of Revolution, the *other faction* disturbs by its very existence the civil peace that would otherwise prevail among the citizens of the world. If there were no kings, no military commanders, no representatives of Big Business, there would be no war. Of course the citizens of the world are grouped into diverse peoples, each one with its own traditions and language. In itself, this diversity is quaint but inconsequential, for all individuals are in principle members of the brotherhood of man. But for partisans of the Counterrevolution, the revolutionary camp may speak the language of the Universal, but it is in reality a particular nation with its own interests to advance. There is thus a real *differend* between these two groups. For those who speak the language of the Universal, the protests of people who have been uprooted from the ground of their traditions, habits, and faith are nothing more than reactionary whining. For those who speak the language of the Particular, the great revolutionary principles are nothing more than lies or illusions. The consequence of such a *differend* is that one cannot pass judgment, unless one is willing to deny all legitimacy to the opposite way of thinking. Thus begins the age of the undecidable:

> Thereafter, it will no longer be known whether the law thereby declared is French or human, whether the war conducted in the name of rights is one of conquest or liberation, whether the violence exerted under the title of freedom is repressive or pedagogical (progressive), whether those nations that are not French ought to become French or become human by endowing themselves with Constitutions that conform to the Declaration, be they anti-French. This confusion permitted by the members of the Constituent Assembly and destined to be propagated throughout the historical-political

---

9. Lyotard, *The Differend*, p. 146 (see also p. 66).

world will turn every national or international conflict into an insoluble differend over the legitimacy of authority.[10]

The dialectic of Enlightenment has the same shortcoming that most
modern philosophies do: it is incapable of recognizing the existence of
differends and is therefore unable to take modern conflicts seriously
without willfully giving up rationality. By presenting the conflict as
one between reason and myth, this dialectic necessarily takes a one-
sided view in which all legitimacy is on the side of reason. Reason can
only be opposed by *specious reasons*: mythical "stories" or "acts of
violence." But why then should this rebellion against reason even
arise? Somewhere along the line, reason itself must also have taken on
the characteristics of a kind of mystifying power. In seeking to recognize the importance of modern conflicts, the dialectic of Enlightenment leads us to suspect that perhaps we were too quick to take the
side of reason. For reason has become an illusion and is nowhere to be
found: everything boils down to a struggle among conflicting powers.

Yet the entire dialectic of Reason and its Other rests on a dubious
opposition. Critical theory sets in opposition *reason* and *tradition* as
two forms of legitimation. This distinction is taken from the sociological typology worked out by Max Weber. In some societies the legitimacy of institutions is traditional: "it has always been the way it is,"
we are told, and that is why it must remain the way it is. In our society,
legitimacy is *rational*: it must be the way it is, and not another way, by
virtue of some principle or law from which the case at hand is derived.
For the sociologist this distinction is, or should be, descriptive. It is one
way of describing the diversity of *reasons* people from different cultures are wont to give for their institutions: in the one case, reasons of
custom or tradition; in the other, reasons drawn from the codes
worked out by experts, legal scholars, and administrators. The sociologist seeks to account for the practices of a culture. But the philosopher
necessarily uses the word "reason" with a normative coloring. For
him, reasons are either good or bad. The sociologist's distinction between reason and tradition is thus for him a *dialectical* one in which
our method of justifying by reasons is opposed to *their* method of

---

10. Ibid., p. 147 [translation modified].

justifying by the absence of reasons. In this view, to found institutions on tradition is to found them on the absence of a foundation, that is, on the simple fact that they already exist. From its descriptive origins, the theory has become critical. Before even setting about describing anything, critical theory begins by establishing that the method of justifying a state of affairs by reasons drawn from tradition is fraudulent. These so-called reasons justify nothing at all. An institution has not yet been justified, if the only thing one can say in its defense is that it has existed for a long time or even forever.

However, by becoming critical, theory gives up the right to make use of the typology derived from comparative sociology. For critical theory, there is no longer anything to compare, since the only things set in opposition are, on the one hand, the true legitimacy that results from our methods and, on the other hand, the irrational or mythical legitimacy that results from every other method. A truly comparative sociologist must be prepared to say, for example, "in this traditional society, people believe that the more traditional an institution is, the more *rational* it is" (i.e., the more in conformity with their requirements for intellectual satisfactoriness). What he is *not* allowed to say is: "in this traditional society, people are satisfied with irrational explanations and mystifying justifications."

What we need, in order to come up with a nondialectical conception of the postmodern and the *differends* that divide it, is to recover the sociological meaning of the "rationalization" that Max Weber labeled *Entzauberung* [disenchantment]. It has sometimes been proposed that this word be translated as "depoeticization." This translation is less than satisfactory for the sociologist who wants to remain faithful to Max Weber's intentions, yet it does give a better idea of what the word is often used to mean. This difference in meaning is indicative of the difficulty that a contemporary mind has in taking up a sociological perspective. It is strange that even Raymond Aron, a Weberian author who fully accepted the idea that we live in a "disenchanted world," provided an explanation of the concept in which one can hear a vaguely romantic undertone.

> The universe in which we live is characterized by what he [Weber] calls *Entzauberung der Welt*, the disenchantment of the world. Sci-

ence has accustomed us to regard external reality as so many blind forces which we can make use of, but nothing remains of the spells, the mirages, the gods, and the fairies which the primitive mind saw all around it. Moreover, in this world stripped of its charms, robbed of meaning and personality, human societies are developing toward an organization that is increasingly rational and bureaucratic.[11]

Here the word "charms" is to be taken in a poetic sense, not a super-natural one. In Aron's explanation primitive thought is limited to forms of expression that, for us, are lacking in seriousness, ones that poetically populate the world with all manner of fanciful denizens. Implicit in this view is the idea that a disenchanted world is a world that is more real, albeit a bit boring. The disenchanted world no longer speaks, it no longer tells us anything. Aron here provides an example of the literary conception that sees myth as a naive explanation of the natural world. If our first encounters with myth took place when studying the ancient classics in school, then we probably view myth as a fable in which each god was associated with a force of nature: there was a god of thunder, an ocean god, etcetera. These gods constituted a poor explanation of things, and it is the first task of reason to repudi-ate them. But in this literary reconstruction of myth, the sacred powers are innocuous. In their "fairylike wondrousness" they make for an "enchanting" background. They are more like the naiads and nymphs of a water ballet at Vaux-le-Vicomte or Versailles, than the chthonic and uranic forces of the original myth. This world before disenchant-ment is a little too close to the world we had to abandon in growing up: the world of Santa Claus, of good fairies, of credulity.

And yet, an enchanted world cannot contain good fairies unless it also contains bad ones. If a peasant from the Bocage discovers that a spell has been put on him (his cows die inexplicably, his wheat is not growing, his wife becomes sick), he is not overjoyed by the fact that the world has finally broken its silence.[12] He is not "charmed," in the sense in which we city dwellers use the term, to be no longer left to himself

---

11. Raymond Aron, *Main Currents in Sociological Thought*, trans. Richard Howard and Helen Weaver (New York: Basic Books, 1967), II, 243–44.

12. See Jeanne Favret-Saada, *Deadly Words: Witchcraft in the Bocage*, trans. Cather-ine Cullen (Cambridge: Cambridge University Press, 1980).

surrounded by mute nature. Instead, it concerns him and he sets about looking for someone to remove the spell. The peasant who thus seeks a remedy to his misfortune through disenchantment, clearly has a different conception of disenchantment than the one provided earlier. Because this conception is part and parcel of the enchanted world, we should perhaps begin with it in order to have an authentically sociological conception of what is at stake in both *Zauber* and *Entzauberung*. In a disenchanted world one calls a veterinarian for one's cows, an agronomist for one's wheat, and a doctor for one's family members. By contrast, in an enchanted world one calls a single person to remedy all three, to remedy the coincidence of all three misfortunes.

Here it may be worthwhile to consult the article "Enchantment" in the *Dictionnaire de théologie catholique*.[13] Unlike the philosopher, the theologian is immediately concerned with putting things in their proper place. For him enchantment is not a mere belief, or a primitive attempt to explain natural phenomena or a prescientific vision of the world. Enchantment is an *operation upon* and not a *representation of* nature. As the author of the article insists, enchantment is *incantatio*, the art of obtaining miracles through song. It is a kind of *magic*, one that should not be understood in the metaphorical (and usually overblown) sense the word is given in classical poetry, but as a magic that accounts for the evil forces that seek our ruin. The theologian who wrote the article is able to provide a list of the different types of magic (those recognized by the Church): charms, enchantments, divination, evocations, fascination, hexes, and spells. What all these practices have in common is that they are a kind of speech that attempts to bring something about. Here we rejoin the analyses of the ethnographer: "Witchcraft is spoken words; but these spoken words are power, and not knowledge or information."[14] But this *power* is less a power over nature than it is a power over *people*. Rationalist anthropology—that of Frazer, for example—sees magic as a sort of imaginary technology, a set of signs by which one hopes to obtain immediate results without going to the trouble of working to produce them. Everywhere that this

---

13. C. Antoine, "Enchantement," *Dictionnaire de théologie catholique*, 1939 ed.

14. Favret-Saada, *Deadly Words*, p. 9.

interpretation looks, it sees only relations between man and nature. What it overlooks are the relations among human beings. For an enchanted world is one in which the first question to be asked after misfortune strikes is: "There wouldn't happen to be anyone out to get you, would there?"[15]

In general, it is difficult to see how a theory of *Entzauberung* could be delineated without making reference to words like "suffering," "uneasiness," "danger," "risk," "distress," "fault," "enemy," and "perdition," or to corresponding words like "remedy," "cure," "salvation," "security," "relief," "offerings and atonement," "aid," "prayer," etcetera. Theories of religion are usually built on an Enlightenment presupposition: *reason* is opposed to *myth*, for myth is only *fable* and fable is worthless as an explanation of nature. According to this view, the intelligent path is the one that leads from religion to science (even if fable does have greater aesthetic value, for it presents the world as a *beautiful whole*, where science sees only indifferent *chaos*). What these theories of religion overlook is the fact that magico-religious practices obviously constitute responses to the idea of the *possibility of misfortune*. The rationalist theory of religion obscures the fact that people are also motivated by concerns like these: "Will I have many offspring?"; "What will happen to my loved ones after I'm gone?"; "Will I accomplish the task?"; "What will happen to me on my journey?" Protection from evil is the real issue. It is thus with this—and not with the rise of Galilean physics—that we must begin if we hope to describe the variety of the "enchanted" world.

Of course the disenchantment of the world has an intellectual aspect, one that can even be provided with a philosophical principle: "there are no mysterious incalculable forces that come into play," and "one can, in principle, master all things by calculation."[16] This definition from Max Weber contains in germ the entire critique of Western metaphysics as "the metaphysics of Being as the calculable and masterable."

---

15. This is the formula for the diagnosis of an enchantment cited ibid., p. 8 [translation modified].

16. Max Weber, "Science as a Vocation," in *From Max Weber*, ed. and trans. H. H. Gerth and C. Wright Mills (New York: Oxford University Press, 1946), p. 139.

But if we stay within such a definition, one that reduces the problem to one of epistemology and the representation of nature, we find ourselves within a dialectic of Enlightenment. For the laws of nature that the partisans of the demystification of the world take to be authoritative are themselves a countermythology that aims to eliminate primitive mythology. The mythology of reason comes to replace the mythology of superstition. As Wittgenstein put it: "The whole modern conception of the world is founded on the illusion that the so-called laws of nature are the explanations of natural phenomena. . . . Thus people today stop at the laws of nature, treating them as something inviolable, just as God and Fate were treated in past ages."[17] It would never occur to an *Aufklärer* to ask himself: "Who is out to get me?" Or at least, he does not ask this question as long as he strives to represent everything that happens to him as a natural phenomenon. For he cannot allow events to be provided with a human signification. He prefers to understand them as a play of natural forces and not as drama. The *Aufklärer* wants to know the mechanisms by which the effects he observes have been produced. He therefore sensibly agrees to limit his reasoning to questions that can be answered using scientific methods. However, by so constraining his inquiry, he allows an Other of reason to be constituted. He cedes part of himself to the unknown, that part of the world that is unfathomable for human consciousness: destiny, misfortune, bad luck, mishap, calamity.[18]

The philosophical principle of disenchantment, as formulated by Max Weber, contains two distinct conceptions of the Enlightenment. The first is ambitious and Promethean: "human calculation"—understood as the ability to treat any situation as a problem to be analyzed into "factors" whose "relations" indicate, according to "formulas" confirmed by science, "solutions" among which it is our job to choose—is all-powerful. This means that human calculation will succeed in what was always the province of magic, a province where magic's powers were not always demonstrable. Calculation is conceived as magic's com-

---

17. Ludwig Wittgenstein, *Tractatus Logico-Philosophicus*, trans. D. F. Pears and B. F. McGuinness (London: Routledge and Kegan Paul, 1961), propositions 6.371 and 6.372.

18. See Edmond Ortigues, "Le destin des oracles" in his *Religions du livre, religions de la coutume* (Paris: Le Sycomore, 1981), pp. 39–57.

petition. The Enlightenment is here in possession of a true myth and real magic. And this is necessarily how the Enlightenment discourse would be understood in the village, the Bocage, or the bush.

The other conception is judicious and modest: the realm of "fate," "chance," and "fortune" begins where "calculation" fails—where, as a result, nothing is to be done. By this conception, misfortune is meaningless. In her book on witchcraft in the Bocage, Jeanne Favret-Saada brings to light the *differend* that exists between the superstitious and the enlightened perspectives. The enlightened mind prefers to interpret magical practices in terms of belief: they are the inevitable consequences of a defective physical theory. The superstitious mind, on the other hand, knows that it is tormented, and asks that someone explain its misfortune to it. Here those who profess to speak the "discourse of modernity" not only seem to deny the validity of the explanation of the problem by way of witchcraft, but also deny that there is anything wrong in the first place. What the superstitious mind sees as a calamity that must be accounted for, the modern mind fails to see at all. In the village the local agent of the Enlightenment—a doctor or teacher—starts out by separating nature and man. On the one hand are the things to be "calculated"; on the other, human relations. Once this separation has been accepted, it becomes impossible for the villager to claim to be someone or something's victim when things go badly for him. The local agent of the Enlightenment thus invites the villager to learn to isolate himself—a self—from his general context: if his rabbits start to die, his rabbits are the ones who are stricken, not he; if his daughter's family breaks up, it is her problem and not his. The villager has to become a modern man, which means that whenever he feels stricken by bad luck he should, like Medea, say: "I still have one thing: me."[19] Like the Fichtean or romantic "Ego," the villager must learn

---

19. This is how Paul Veyne has aptly summed up what a modern morality of caring for oneself would be. The dictum of Corneille's Medea reads:

> Me,
> Me, I say, and that's enough.

See Paul Veyne, "Le dernier Foucault et sa morale," *Critique*, nos. 471–72 (1986), p. 939.

irony: in reality, he identifies with no mere "finite determination." But by the same token he appears to set himself up as an *invulnerable subject,* one that is invulnerable in its elusiveness. Everything that happens ends up happening to the Non-Ego. Nothing can harm the Ego. In such a situation, rationalist discourse itself enters into a magical dimension of removing curses and fighting witchcraft, a dimension of *disenchantment* understood as an operation to counteract misfortune, eliminate bad luck, and guarantee salvation. For every definition of witchcraft begins with the idea that the potential victim of magic is he who is vulnerable to misfortune: he may be attacked because he is of this world, because he owns things that can be ruined, because he is involved in enterprises that can be disrupted, because he has a family that depends on him. By asking the villager to think of his *self* as situated someplace other than in his house, his land, his harvest, or his family, the *Aufklärer* seems to the villager to deny the possibility that he himself (and no other) can be harmed by an attack on what is dear to him. Such a villager will hardly believe his ears: this house, these cows, this wife, these children—none of this is *him.* He is invited to see these things as foreign to him, as a Non-Ego. Better yet, he must see things this way if he hopes to be an infinite Ego. But the idea of becoming an infinite Ego may strike him as somewhat inhuman.

What, then, are we to make of the war between philosophy (reason) and myth (the Other of reason)? We simply do not believe in it, for we remember Aristotle's dictum: "kai o philomuthos philosophos pōs esti" (the lover of myths is in a sense a philosopher).[20] Myth is not the Other of reason, it is merely another domain of human reason. In this domain of mythological reason, restrictions have not yet been placed on the exercise of reason, for it is out of such restrictions that what seems to be an Other of reason arises. One is still allowed to be amazed by chance, by coincidence, by strange regularities, by extraordinary accidents, by significant correspondences, and the like. The rationality of myth is too rich for philosophical stomachs that can only digest it if it has been diluted, amended, and enhanced by metaphysical distinctions: the possible and the necessary, the essential and the acci-

---

20. Aristotle, *Metaphysics,* I, 982^b19.

dental, the ontological and the empirical, the intelligible and the sensible, etcetera. But philosophical rationality is still too dense and too concentrated for the taste of our science, which insists that one first establish the conditions of a possible solution before one sets about posing problems. The good old "law of the three stages" (of the evolution of the human mind) does not move from primitive irrationality to modern rationality: rather, it moves from a *condensed and thick* rationality ["une rationalité épaisse"] to a *clear* one (in the sense in which water is clear).

> First of all, men did not begin thinking when they invented, in Greece, what the classicists call a "consistent discourse." The invention must have consisted of a *decomposition*: the different dimensions of existence were separated out, each in a distinct sequence of discourse. Rational discourse says one thing at a time, while the myth or the poem makes allusion to all in one sentence. The one is flat, the other is "thick." . . . Philosophical rationality still aims at totality, even if this is a totality stripped of its thickness, so to speak. Scientific rationality, which predominates among the moderns, aims each time at a slice of totality. It is essentially instrumental (relating means to ends) and specialized in the sense that it operates within compartments that are not rationally but empirically defined.[21]

---

21. Louis Dumont, "The Anthropological Community and Ideology," trans. Alan McConnell Duff and Louis Dumont, in *Essays on Individualism* (Chicago: University of Chicago Press, 1986), p. 220.

=== 7 ===

The Project of Autonomy

> Esperanto. The feeling of disgust we get if we utter an *invented* word with invented derivative syllables. The word is cold, lacking in associations, and yet it plays at being "language."
>
> Wittgenstein, *Culture and Value*[1]

Modern culture gives rise to a difficulty of which contemporary philosophy is more often an expression than a part of the remedy. Each time that we oppose *reason* and *tradition*, we express our culture's intense drive toward innovation, experimentation, and ingenuity. Sociologists call this drive toward novelty for its own sake *individualism*. As a matter of principle, we prefer situations where individuals have a choice over situations where their environment feeds them all the answers to the questions they have never even had a chance to ask. For us, the best of all worlds is one in which each of us has the *burden of choice*. The idea of doing things the way they have always been done strikes us as being simply a matter of laziness. And it seems absurd to us for someone to do things the way they have always been done for no other reason than that they have always been done that way. We think of people who take tradition as their rule as being like children: they have not yet reached the age where reason becomes active.

The opposition of reason and tradition is more a philosophical proverb about culture than a well-thought-out philosophical maxim. In reality, it is quite difficult to provide a coherent meaning to this antithesis. We have been told that reason and tradition are two ways of

---

1. Ludwig Wittgenstein, *Culture and Value*, ed. G. H. von Wright and Heikki Nyman, trans. Peter Winch (Chicago: University of Chicago Press, 1980), p. 52.

legitimating customs and institutions. Though we can understand how reason is a source of legitimacy, we have trouble seeing how there can be any other such sources. How can legitimation be based on anything other than reason, for example, on tradition or inspiration (charisma)? We would seem to be faced with a legitimation by a legitimate principle of legitimation on the one hand, and legitimation by an illegitimate principle on the other. Our typology would then have to distinguish between a legitimation that legitimizes and one that, devoid of legitimizing power, is nevertheless a form of legitimation.

Only one philosophy has proven capable of drawing out the consequences of the opposition between individual reason, on the one hand, and everything that an external authority provides, transmits, translates, or presents as given to the individual, on the other. This philosophy is *empiricism*, a doctrine that acknowledges only one legitimate source of valid assertions: *my* experience. This is evident in the standard textbook example: I have the right to say that all the Englishwomen *that I have seen* have been redheads, but I do not have the right to say that all Englishwomen *are* redheads. It is widely recognized that this philosophy, in the attempt to remodel the world on a solipsistic basis, ends up with a world suited only for philosophers, a hypothetical construction in which sense data—the immediate elements of consciousness—are only indistinctly connected to one another. This philosophy founders on the so-called problem of induction, a problem that empiricism creates for itself through its initial epistemological axiom. For nothing in my experience assures me that the redheads were even English. After all, I wasn't around to see them born in England of English parents. I have never even seen their parents nor, for that matter, have I seen England *as such*: I have only seen a few streets, parks, and pubs. Moreover, I have no way of knowing whether the redheads remain redheads when I am not around. My experience turns out to be quite limited. As a result, everything that I believed I knew from experience will have to be reformulated: I did not *know* it, I merely ventured a hypothesis regarding the perpetuation of the regularity I had observed in the past. Serious attempts at formulating an empiricist philosophy have seen this way of thinking as a correction of our everyday idea of experience rather than as an attempt to ground knowledge in experience in the usual sense. For what we usually call experience includes tradition: observations made by other members of our society, books written by our authors, the teachings of our masters, the anonymous wisdom of our language. The subject of this experience is a collective one. The considerable efforts that have been made, from Hume to the Vienna Circle, to individualize this subject have resulted in an important finding for philosophy: they have proven that it is strictly impossible to rework collective empirical knowledge into individual empirical knowledge.

When a philosopher attempts to individualize authority—the source of legitimation—to the furthest extent possible, he is in his own way making a contribution to the realization of the *project of autonomy* that is the veritable content of the "modern project." But the same philosopher is simply expressing his culture when he takes it on himself to pose the "problem of values." In truth, this so-called problem is less a problem that might eventually be solved than a concentrated expression of the tensions of our culture. We can be certain in advance that anyone who takes on the "problem of values" will either remain satisfied with a pseudosolution or admit defeat. For the problem is set up in such a way as to be insoluble. All the solutions that one might provide are excluded in advance by the very formulation of the problem. What, then, is the content of this problem? We are told that it is a matter of justifying values, of finding a foundation for them. An individual who has the *burden of choice* acquits himself of it through an appeal to criteria of excellence or of opportunity. Those around him use other criteria. But what is now at issue is an explanation of the choice of the criteria themselves. Thus, in the formulation of the problem of values, the word "value" indicates that the decision is up to the individual, that his dignity and responsibility are at stake. Yet in the same formulation, the word "foundation" indicates that all choices are not equivalent. Some choices are clearly poor, even criminal. It follows that there is a general possibility of reasoning about the value of a choice. But valid reasoning applies to everyone. From this point on, the individual consciousness is no longer the ultimate authority when it comes to evaluation. It must no longer be *Consciousness*, but *Reason* or the *Concept* that decides things, since we have just established that one's personal preferences are powerless to turn a crime into an act of good, or a stupid decision into a stroke of genius. And here, the now-bewildered philosopher can go no further. Indeed, he finds himself on the verge of forswearing the use of the word "value." He is tempted to subordinate the freedom of consciousness to a superior authority, one that may be transcendental but is surely inhuman.

In short, if there are values, they cannot be grounded, and if they are grounded, they are not values. Can we even say: "There *are* values"? No, we must not. For if we have grown accustomed to talking about value, it is precisely as a way of excluding the possibility that values exist *out there*, of refusing the eventuality that there be something in the world that corresponds to our value judgments. If there were values, they would exist without our having any say in the matter. But having reached this point, the contemporary philosopher may rightfully be concerned that the most profound questions of existence have come to resemble questions of taste. We say: "What really exists is not, for example, good spinach, but rather spinach, and someone—me—who likes it mushy, steamed, and so on." By speaking in this way, we have encouraged relativism ("everyone has his own values"), historicism ("each age has its own values"), and nihilism ("in itself, nothing has value").

In response, philosophy becomes rationalist. A rationalist begins by endorsing the modern project of individual autonomy, a project that rationalism did not invent (and here it cannot be overemphasized that the most qualified and vigorous representative of modern thought is neither the rationalist with his principle of sufficient reason, nor the idealist and his "Spirit," but the empiricist and his epistemology of sensory ideas). Thus each person is enjoined from imposing *his own* values on others. Indeed, how would he be able to justify such an act? The very notion of value is designed to allow one to denounce the tyranny that ensues each time a single individual seeks to dictate everybody else's choices in accordance with his own particular preferences. And yet, according to the rationalist, all is not lost. One need only make a distinction between the set of my "preferences" that are indeed subjective (my "empirical" tastes, whims, and inclinations) and another group of "preferences" that are truly rational. I have the right to impose the latter on others because I myself have had them imposed on me, not by some domineering tyrant, but by the disinterested reason that alone awakens us all to our true freedom.

Rationalist philosophy hopes to provide a commanding rational basis for the moral constraints that were formerly imposed on individuals by the social bonds of an ordered society. The "moral obligation" of which it speaks is the interiorized form of the previous social subordination.[2] Countless *theories of justice* have been formulated in which philosophers have attempted to show how a proper application of the principle of contradiction to the problems involved in the organization of a society allows one to present an entire set of moral and political principles (the basic rights of man, the rules of reciprocity, certain forms of solidarity, etc.) as the product of impartial reason rather than of some "interested" empirical subject. It is somewhat unsettling, however, when one comes to the realization that the rational framework of a human society of autonomous individuals bears such a strong resemblance to the rules governing discussion clubs and *sociétés de pensée*. Here again we encounter a model of social experience patterned on the Republic of Letters, an idea whose power over the minds of the eighteenth century has been demonstrated by Reinhart Koselleck.

Though philosophers may make reference to a modern *project*, whenever they articulate this project, they give the impression that they see it as already having been accomplished. Purely reciprocal social bonds would have to be *intersubjective* bonds, each *ego* having as its counterpart an *alter ego* for which it is in turn the *alter ego*. By virtue of this reciprocity, the equitable distribution of available resources—whether the benefits of some communal endeavor or the allotted time at the lectern during a debate—must come about of itself through a freely formed consensus. The people that the philosopher links to one another with intersubjective bonds have no *social* identity: they are not parents or children, physicians or patients, legitimate rulers or subjects, experts or apprentices, notables or jesters. Their relations with one another are thus in no way social. They merely *communicate*, like colleagues at some scientific convention, or *cooperate*, under conditions that they have put in place themselves, like the partners in a joint venture (i.e., a *societas* as defined in Roman law).

---

2. Louis Dumont, *From Mandeville to Marx* (Chicago: University of Chicago Press, 1977), p. 54.

Cornelius Castoriadis points out that "activities that aim at [the] autonomy" of oneself and of everyone else—activities that are and must continue to be for us the highest calling conceivable—present serious philosophical and political difficulties precisely because the social cannot be reduced to the intersubjective.[3] The crucial point is that societies acquire a *collective identity* in their particular culture, a culture that, at least ideologically, provides a coherence that no intersubjectivity can. The whole of modern anthropology serves to show that culture is a real system and not the momentary result of a myriad of individual interactions among "subjects" each of whom has his own personal life-style.

> In studying an archaic society, at times one has the staggering sensation that a team of psychoanalysts, economists, sociologists, etc., possessing superhuman capacities and knowledge, has already worked on the problem of its coherence and has dictated a series of rules to ensure this coherence.[4]

The image of a team of experts working together to build a coherent society, and a primitive one at that, immediately brings to mind the—usually ill-fated—efforts of bureaucratic "commissions" assigned the task of drawing up the plan for an entire neighborhood, a public building, or even a new vehicle. By itself, the rational discussion of collective problems often results in nothing more than unimaginative compromises. But Castoriadis's fictional intersubjective committee would seem to be haunted by the inspiring figure of the Philosopher-Legislator. If our laws are good ones, only a Sage of superhuman abilities could have drafted them. The notion is Rousseau's:

> To discover the rules of society that are best suited to nations, there would need to exist a superior intelligence. . . . Whoever ventures on the enterprise of setting up a people must be ready, shall we say, to change human nature. . . . It is this which has obliged the founders of nations throughout history to appeal to divine intervention

---

3. Cornelius Castoriadis, "Individual, Society, Rationality, History," in *Philosophy, Politics, Autonomy*, ed. and trans. David Ames Curtis (New York: Oxford University Press, 1991), p. 77.

4. Cornelius Castoriadis, *The Imaginary Institution of Society*, trans. Kathleen Blamey (Cambridge, Mass.: MIT Press, 1987), p. 47.

and to attribute their own wisdom to the Gods; for then the people, feeling subject to the laws of the state as they are to those of nature . . . obey freely and bear with docility the yoke of the public welfare.[5]

Rousseau's interpretation of religion here is *political*. In his view, religion's primary function is to found institutions. It is a political instrument. But the entire text of the *Social Contract*, with its legendary figure of the wise Legislator, shows the extent to which we are unable to imagine *the institution of a people* without appealing to more familiar models like the adoption of a bill of law by the Legislator, a contractual agreement signed by two or more parties, or the instructions given to newcomers by the founders. We act as though the question of the group's collective identity somehow precedes the answer that the group itself gives. But a group devoid of collective identity is *not* what Rousseau refers to as a *people*, a group that can either conserve its own institutions or adopt new ones as a way of modernizing. Castoriadis characterizes this intellectual difficulty in the following way:

> Every society up to now has attempted to give an answer to a few fundamental questions: Who are we as a collectivity? What are we for one another? Where and in what are we? What do we want; what do we desire; what are we lacking? Society must define its "identity." Without the "answer" to these "questions," without these "definitions," there can be no human world, no society, no culture—for everything would be an undifferentiated chaos.[6]

If we remove the quotation marks from this text, we have an exact representation of the modern philosophical perspective on the institution of society. By this view we imagine a group of *orators* who, in a spirit of free deliberation, pronounce *eloquent speeches* for the consideration of the *assembled people*. But where did the orators learn the art of rhetoric? Who taught them to speak? How was the assembly convened? How was the matter for debate decided upon? We should

5. Jean-Jacques Rousseau, *The Social Contract*, book II, chapter 7, trans. Maurice Cranston (New York: Penguin, 1968), pp. 84–87.

6. Castoriadis, *The Imaginary Institution of Society*, pp. 146–47.

obviously reinstate the quotation marks and admit that we were only speaking metaphorically, figurally.

> These are not questions and answers that are posed explicitly, and the definitions are not ones given in language. The questions are not even raised prior to the answers. Society constitutes itself by producing a *de facto* answer to these questions in its life, in its activity. It is in the *doing* of each collectivity that the answer to these questions appears as an embodied meaning.[7]

The inevitable question then arises of knowing what we can say about the institution of a people if we want to avoid speaking metaphorically. Here Castoriadis introduces the philosophical term "auto-institution." The use of such a concept entails certain paradoxes that have been well known since Fichte's use of the concept of *self-positing* [*das Sichselbstsetzen*]. These paradoxes can be expressed as follows:

1. *Either* the concept of self-positing marks a distinction, proposes a goal, and has a certain critical value, in which case it serves to condemn every existing form of humanity in such a way that the project of autonomy becomes utopian,
2. *or* the concept is a metaphysical one and is thus of no use in choosing a form of existence, but rather serves to specify the ontological status of the human (the "I" is not posited by something else, nor does it posit something other than itself, it is self-positing), in which case it follows that everything human, regardless of its shape and form, necessarily satisfies what has thus been established as the condition of possibility for being human.

The average French reader has not read Fichte. Yet another form of the preceding difficulty is familiar to him: one need only pose the problem in Sartrian terms as the opposition between authenticity and bad faith. "Self-positing" is then renamed the "fundamental existential project." If we take the notion of radical freedom in a moral sense, we should then be able to define the only honest moral project: to live unwaveringly in accordance with our radical freedom. Every other project is to be denounced, for none of them takes the risks of radical

---

7. Ibid., p. 147.

freedom. Yet it soon becomes apparent that everyone is thereby condemned, for each of us has acquiesced in alienation of one form or
another. As a result, the moral project becomes utopian. But at the
same time, the existentialist notion of a radical choice of the values
and meaning of life begins to take on a metaphysical cast in which it is
no longer a *possibility* but the very *mark* of the human condition. In
the metaphysician's view, man as such takes on the status of being
causa sui. From that point on, whether man wallows in alienation or
participates in struggles for liberation, he cannot but exhibit his ontological condition. This is the predictable result of metaphysical reduplication. Man as such, *qua homo*, is the being that chooses what it will
be through the choice of a supreme value: thus the atheist existentialist
has chosen radical freedom where the Christian existentialist has just
as radically chosen the "Hidden God," and the Marxist has radically
chosen dialectical Matter where the structuralist has chosen subjectless
Process.

Castoriadis also runs into this difficulty. For him, a heteronomous
society is one in which the Legislator, to use Rousseau's terms, presents
his own wisdom as that of the Gods. An autonomous society is one in
which the Legislator is held to be identical with the sovereign people,
one in which the people is able to provide its own collective identity
through a sovereign act in which, by answering the question "Who are
we?," it knows itself to be expressing its own will and not that of the
Gods or some universal order of things. The autonomous society—at
one and the same time democratic and free from any transcendent
authority—is one in which *we* decide. One might then be led to believe
that such a society is also one that achieves self-positing, one that institutes itself. In other words, societies are heteronomous when people
allow their collective identity to be determined by the past, by history,
by tradition, by the Gods, and so on. Heteronomous collective identity
would thus seem to be a determination by something other than oneself,
along the lines of the traditional formula: we are the inadequate descen-
dants of superior Ancestors. Only an autonomous collective identity
would then provide an example of a determination of and by oneself. A
"We" that starts out "infinite" or indeterminate posits itself by freely
providing itself with the determinate identity of its choice. This conception of autoinstitution, which is *not* that of Castoriadis, leads directly to

a utopian view. An autonomous society is a goal that can only be attained through a passage *out of* history. A society will only be self-positing the day it no longer allows itself to be determined by its past, its traditions, its examples and circumstances. Here we are reminded of the twentieth-century brand of millenarian prophesying: something is coming, an *Ereignis* that will hurl us forward into a new age; we are about to cross the frontier. Though these exalted expectations of a revolutionary break—a kind of Western version of the Cargo Cult[8]—draw their vocabulary from philosophy, they fail to make the important distinctions among ethics, politics, and metaphysics.

But Castoriadis's understanding of self-positing is not that of the millenarians. For him, self-positing is the condition of every human institution. Castoriadis's position is thus that of a consistent metaphysician. Every human institution has been created, insofar as none of them is derived from either the imitation of natural models or some transcendental archetype. Some societies institute themselves *as* heteronomous: they choose to have Gods, sacred laws, an inviolable order of things. Western society, on the other hand, is engaged in a painful struggle to secure an autonomous basis for itself.

> Society is autocreation. Its institution is an autoinstitution that it has thus far hidden from itself. This auto-occultation is precisely the fundamental characteristic of the heteronomy of societies. . . . In other words, in them the institution of the society is presented to the individuals as not being their affair; they are led to believe that they cannot give themselves their own law—for that is what "autonomy" means—but that this law has already been handed down by someone else.[9]

The difficulty here is that we must now make a distinction between societies that seek to subject themselves to a transcendent Legislator and those that seek to give themselves their own law. Here again we come across the paradoxes of Rousseau's *Social Contract* and German idealism. On the one hand, we have the impossible operation of the free alienation of one's own liberty (the slave freely chooses servitude,

---

8. See Kenelm Burridge, *New Heaven, New Earth: A Study of Millenarian Activities* (Oxford: Basil Blackwell, 1969).

9. Cornelius Castoriadis, *Domaines de l'homme* (Paris: Seuil, 1986), p. 315.

the heteronomous society institutes itself *as* having been instituted by someone or something other than itself). On the other hand, we have the almost inconceivable act of alienating *oneself to oneself* (each individual surrenders totally to the community, and the community gives back equal membership in the community). These antithetical operations end up resembling one another: *the liberty that accepts subordination* is opposed to *the subordination that liberates*, but at the same time the two are strangely related. Castoriadis here makes a distinction between autonomy and autoinstitution. Autonomy is a clearheaded autoinstitution, while heteronomy is an autoinstitution that has been occulted. Even so, if one can choose to give oneself God's will rather than the will of the people as one's law, isn't autoinstitution in the end the same thing as autonomy? Moreover, such a definition is approximately that of the ordinary use of the word "autonomy" in political vocabulary. When a group claims its autonomy, it demands to have its collective identity respected. "Autonomists" are those who want to speak their own national language rather than a foreign one, to conserve their own laws rather than have others imposed on them, to maintain their own religion and customs, etcetera. As a modern philosopher, Castoriadis considers a people heteronomous if it has made an alliance with God or respects the law of its Ancestors. But the people themselves do not see things this way: the God is *their* God, the God of *their* Ancestors. Were Castoriadis to go about trying to prescribe his definition of autonomy to a heteronomous people, they would protest what they would see as the imposition of a foreign collective identity on everything that confirms them as the people they are. They would see Castoriadis as a kind of Jacobin. But even the French Republicans, in their romantic phase, enthusiastically proclaimed the principle of nationhood during the so-called "printemps des peuples" [springtime of nations] of 1848. They saw this principle as the purest expression of the project of autonomy. In the end, modern nationalism asserts the same right to autonomy as does the federalist socialism of Proudhon or, for that matter, Castoriadis. Heidegger himself did not have to look far to find justification for Hitler's various international showdowns: he appealed to the unconditional demand for autonomy. When the Führer sought to pull Germany from the League of Nations, Heidegger approved this demonstration of "the clear will to unconditional self-responsibility in enduring and mastering the fate of our people."[10] These are all signs that the concept of autonomy is always understood in the metaphysical sense of being a characteristic of the "human condition," a "condemnation to freedom." And this means that it can no longer be used to characterize only certain choices and certain forms of identity rather than all of them.

Castoriadis undoubtedly knows all this, for he says that autonomy is not the ultimate political answer. We seek autonomy, but what do we want to do with it?[11] In the absence of an answer to this question, we risk lapsing into a Kantian sort of formalism. In itself, democracy is not the last word. For a democratic political regime requires another regime—one of *customs and mores*—in its support.

> It is impossible to draw up a constitution that, for example, forbids the possibility that one day 67 percent of the individuals will make the "democratic" decision to deprive the other 33 percent of their rights. A Constitution may contain inalienable individual rights, but it cannot contain a clause absolutely forbidding the revision of the Constitution itself. If such a clause were put in, it would sooner or later prove ineffectual. The only essential limitation that can be placed on a democracy is a self-limitation. This, in turn, can only be a job for individuals educated within, by, and for democracy.[12]

Thus the autoinstitution by means of a solemn *decision* made by the assembled citizenry is not the last word. The last word is rather "autolimitation," a self-limitation through the formation of customs. In other words, modern democratic societies are unique in having found *in themselves* the power to limit themselves, instead of ascribing this power to majestic institutions requiring a kind of worship or piety, as was the case not only in ancient democracies but in the Enlightenment-era American form of democracy as well. Our path thus crosses that of sociologists from Tocqueville to Louis Dumont. Castoriadis writes:

---

10. In the text already cited in chapter 5 (n. 34), *New German Critique*, no. 45 (1988), p. 103.

11. Castoriadis, *Domaines de l'homme*, p. 416.

12. Ibid., p. 416.

> As Durkheim understood, religion is "identical" with society at its origins and for some time afterward: in fact, this is true for almost every known society. Almost always and everywhere, the entire organization of the social world is essentially "religious." Religion does not "accompany" or "explain" or "justify" the organization of society: it *is* that organization. . . . Religion organizes, polarizes, and valorizes priorities, arranging them into a *hierarchy* in a sense that is close to the original meaning of this word.[13]

A problem immediately arises for a culture shaped by the project of autonomy. Among the societies participating in this culture, the task of limiting the "infinite" human will can no longer be carried out by institutions based on the *justice of the world*. Indeed, the hubris of an "infinite" will, one that takes itself as its only reference and refuses any and every curb or limitation, is no longer disciplined by a *religion identical to society itself*. In Rousseau's terms: the spiritual and missionary religion of *man* (i.e., Christianity) has supplanted the pagan religion—"enclosed within a single country"—of the *citizen*.[14] In such a circumstance, philosophers are tempted to invest *politics* with the traditional religious function of providing a *hierarchy* to the world in such a way that human action is possible.

Castoriadis continues to cast his project of autonomy as a *politics*, because he believes it is still possible to return to the ancient meaning of the word. He draws a distinction between two uses of the word. In his view, the political [*le politique*] is a specialized category of activities and undertakings that concern the explicit power of a society and its organs of government (and this whether or not there exists a State and, if so, regardless of its form). But in the Greek sense of the word, politics [*la politique*] concerns the entire society and its institution: not only power but, as in Plato's *Politeia*, the division of labor, the relations of kinship,

---

13. Ibid., p. 372.

14. See *The Social Contract*, book IV, chapter 8, "On Civil Religion." Castoriadis's reflections suffer from a failure to give any role to evangelical preaching in forming the project of autonomy. In his view this project, born in the agora of the Greek city-state, simply came to be "reborn" after an intervening period of barbarity. Marcel Gauchet, in a work that (unfortunately, to my mind) seeks to provide a *political* history of religion, has attempted to place the democratic movement within the framework of the religious evolution of humanity. See *Le désenchantement du monde* (Paris: Gallimard, 1985).

education, customs, mores, games, theology, etcetera. It would be nothing short of catastrophic to attempt to understand the project of autonomy, which concerns the totality of society, in the limited modern sense
of the word "political": one would come to the Terroristic conclusion
that "everything is political." As an adjective, "political" in the modern
sense serves to qualify "whatever pertains to explicit and at least partially conscious and reflective decisions concerning the collectivity."[15]
Using this definition, to say that "everything is political" would mean
that the Sovereign, whether the absolutist State or the Revolutionary
Council, is to *decide everything*. "Through a strange reversal, language,
economy, religion, representation of the world, family, etc., have to be
said to depend upon political decisions in a way that would win the
approval of Charles Maurras as well as of Pol Pot."[16] In other words,
totalitarianism cannot be held to be the opposite of democracy without
further qualification, just because it is its adversary and represents its
undoing. Totalitarianism is also the system that is closest to democracy.
It is democracy without autolimitation, or rather, it is the project of
autonomy betrayed and disfigured into the project of a total self-
foundation in the form of an explicit control, an explicit and premedi-
tated decision. Despite the fact that he was at that time still in the thrall
of Marxist dogma, Castoriadis was quick to realize after World War II
that the *same world* bore within it not only the possibility of a humane
society—which, at the time, he called *socialism*—but also the possibility for this project to lapse into *barbarism* [*la barbarie*],[17] an unprecedented barbarism unknown among the former peasants of the Danube.

One might be justified in thinking that the modern sense of the word
"political" has become too well established for us to return to its
ancient meaning. Our concern should be to challenge the tendency to
reduce the social (customs and mores, the ancient *politeia*) to the

---

15. Cornelius Castoriadis, "Power, Politics, Autonomy," in *Philosophy, Politics, Autonomy*, p. 158.

16. Ibid., p. 92.

17. Translator's note: Socialisme ou Barbarie [Socialism or Barbarism] was the name
of a French revolutionary leftist organization founded in 1949 by dissidents of the
French Trotskyist movement; its members included Castoriadis and Claude Lefort. See
Cornelius Castoriadis, *Social and Political Writings*, vol. 1, ed. and trans. David Ames
Curtis (Minneapolis: University of Minnesota Press, 1988).

political in the modern sense of the word (the power and law that are explicitly put in place by an identifiable Legislator). It is just such a reduction that prevents philosophers from thinking about both aspects of the project of autonomy at once: the conscious aspect that is easy to put in philosophical terms, and an aspect that is anthropological and thus inaccessible to rational reconstruction. The implausibility of rationalist doctrines is never so clear as when they treat of political theory. The rationalist thinker acts as though social life takes place entirely in the political arena: he uncovers *strategies, relations of domination,* alliances and struggles for *power.* Louis Dumont demonstrates this in the case of Hobbes: in one movement, the philosopher brushes aside hierarchy and turns all social relations into relations of force.[18] He eliminates hierarchy from his cosmology in order to liberate the individual. But as Castoriadis, following Durkheim, has pointed out, hierarchy is nothing less than the religion organizing society. The modern philosopher does not take a given order of things as his point of departure, but rather begins with a chaos out of which the individuals who encounter one another are meant to forge an order and its concomitant relations of subordination so as to render action possible in the world. Thus it is that modern philosophy gives birth to a social theory that can only understand politics as defined by the legitimate or illegitimate use of violence and the categories of enemy and friend.

> In this theory, the social is to a great measure reduced to the political. Why? The reason is very clear in Hobbes: starting from the *individuum*, or the individual, social life will be necessarily considered in terms of consciousness and force (or "power"). In the first place, one can pass from the individual to the group only in terms of "covenant," i.e., in terms of conscious transaction or artificial design. It will then be a matter of "force," because "force" is the only thing the individual can bring into the bargain: the opposite of "force" would be hierarchy, the idea of the social order, the principle of authority; and this is precisely what the contracting individuals will more or less unconsciously have to bring forth synthetically from the common pool of their forces or wills.[19]

---

18. Louis Dumont, *Essays On Individualism: Modern Ideology in Anthropological Perspective* (Chicago: University of Chicago Press, 1986), pp. 84–85.

19. Ibid., p. 85.

As a result, there is work for contemporary philosophers to do in this area. We would prefer to conceive of human institutions using an idiom which is no longer that of the abstract social theory that passes for modern philosophy's political theory. This theory always sees the origins of such institutions either in explicit conventions agreed to among atomistic subjects, or in the relations of force resulting from a given historical configuration. To arrive at such a new conception, we will have to shake our minds of the hold that the notion of the Philosopher-Legislator has long had on us.

In his *Remarks on Frazer's "Golden Bough,"* Wittgenstein criticized Frazer's narrowly rationalistic explanations of Scottish Beltane festivals. Frazer's error was to see these rituals, which call to mind human sacrifice, as having originated in opinions and beliefs (the falsity of which he thought accounted for the fact that the ritual does not in fact produce the effects that the primitives expect of this "technology"). Wittgenstein sees in this an example of the fallacy that a people is founded by an individual: "[F]estivals of this kind are not so to speak haphazard inventions of one man but need an infinitely broader basis if they are to persist. If I tried to invent a festival, it would very soon die out or else be so modified that it corresponded to a general inclination in people."[20] In order to institute a people, the philosopher would have to be able to invent collective rituals and festivals. But why can't he? Like everyone else, he surely understands that every society has such rituals, though he might well wonder if they are *necessary*. Would we even call "human" a society where the very concept of the ritual or festival is unknown? The philosopher is thus clearly able to philosophize about the fact that there are—that there must be—such rituals and festivals, but he must avoid changing this requirement for festivals—the condition of possibility for life to be human—into some kind of "transcendental festival" (a slippage that phenomenologists have not always proven able to avoid). Above all, what he cannot do is turn from his reflections on festivals in general in order to then invent one in all its details and

20. Ludwig Wittgenstein, *Remarks on Frazer's "Golden Bough,"* ed. Rush Rhees, trans. A. C. Miles and Rush Rhees (Atlantic Highlands, N.J.: Humanities Press, 1979), pp. 16–17.

ceremonies. Wittgenstein thus would have recognized the wisdom of Mauss's objections to the speculations of the College of Sociology: a philosopher is not able to *give rhythm to social life*. In this view, Wittgenstein distances himself from classical rationalism, as Jacques Bouveresse has pointed out: "The idea that man can in some way—by dint of free will and reason alone—create his language and way of life in the same way that he can create something within the framework of an already-established language game and form of life, seemed to him to be totally naive and absurd."[21] It will be said—not without reason—that Wittgenstein is a conservative. But perhaps we are now more disposed to come to terms with his assessments after such episodes of grand modernism as the collectivization of Russian agriculture, the Chinese and Cambodian cultural revolutions, or the "systematization" of the well known Romanian tyrant who proposed leveling old villages and replacing them with well-policed centers of agricultural exploitation.

In an essay on the theme of convention in analytic philosophy, Hilary Putnam sets Wittgenstein in opposition to Carnap.[22] Carnap's positions are classically modern: he is in favor of the conventional, the constructed, the planned. His philosophy, according to Putnam, is part of the same cultural spirit as the Bauhaus and Le Corbusier's Cité radieuse. He thus forms part of modernism's optimistic and generous wing. As for Wittgenstein, he is in Putnam's view just as modern as Carnap, but his modernism is anguished and suffering. Wittgenstein wants to reestablish the legitimacy of the natural, of the traditional, of organic development, of formations that spontaneously arise in the absence of any ambitious total plan. Putnam offers an excellent encapsulation of the difference between the two mindsets. Carnap believes all at once in Esperanto, socialist planning, and the ideal language of science, a kind of mental Cité radieuse. This is why he and the Vienna Circle (and Carnap's disciple Quine, as Putnam points out) were constantly issuing gigantic programs and provocative claims: soon all human knowledge will be reduced to physics; soon physics will be

---

21. Jacques Bouveresse, "L'animal cérémoniel," in Ludwig Wittgenstein, *Remarques sur le "Rameau d'or" de Frazer*, trans. J. Lacoste (Paris: L'âge d'homme, 1982), p. 68.

22. Hilary Putnam, "Convention: A Theme in Philosophy," in his *Philosophical Papers* (Cambridge: Cambridge University Press, 1983), III, 170.

translated into purely factual observations linked to one another by purely logical relations (soon, adds Quine, philosophy and logic will be "naturalized"). This is another example of futurist impatience. For those in the avant-garde of progress, to draw up the program of future triumphs is already half the task. Wittgenstein condemns this forward-looking fervor: the Vienna Circle should not simply proclaim the end of metaphysics, nor make announcements about everything it *will* do; rather, it should *show* what its efforts are able to produce *now*.[23] Wittgenstein is just as modern as Carnap, but is more philosophically discerning. This is why he was so unenthusiastic about massive constructions whose chimerical nature was immediately obvious to him.

Philosophically, how are we to express Wittgenstein's *moderation?* Here modernity consists in recognizing that the rules that humans follow in their thinking (and thus also in their existence) are not the expression of the nature of things. By granting this, Wittgenstein pays his debt to the Moderns' *critical reason.* But another step—a postmodern one, perhaps—is required in order to overcome the Modern illusion by which the *autonomy of rules* (relative to reality) can only be understood in terms of an *autonomy of the individual* that takes as its guide the powerful images of the Legislator and the first Convention.

Wittgenstein explains that philosophers have trouble accounting for *truths of reason* (principles, axioms, necessary rules, universal laws). The empiricist cannot see how such truths could be *extracted* from experience. And he is right: they cannot be arrived at through "abstraction." He therefore tries to reduce them either to pure, empty tautologies or to the most general of hypotheses. The rationalist, on the other hand, cannot see how one could view the principle of contradiction or mathematical theorems as tautologies or hypotheses. And he is right: the empiricist thesis is ultimately impossible to maintain. Those who do, do so not because they find it convincing, but because they think things must be this way if the empiricist epistemological dogma is to be upheld. The rationalist attempts to present truths of reason as a priori knowledge. If he is a phenomenologist, he makes them into eidetic propositions grounded in an intuition of essences. If he is a Kantian, he

---

23. See Wittgenstein's letter to Waismann, cited in Friedrich Waismann, ed., *Wittgenstein und der Wiener Kreis* (Frankfurt: Suhrkamp, 1984), p. 18.

makes them into propositions regarding the transcendental object that are derived from the analysis of the conditions of possibility for the consciousness of any object whatever.

Wittgenstein seeks to demonstrate that what is expected of truths of reason is impossible. They must be *necessary*, that is, valid in all circumstances and in every hypothetical state of affairs. At the same time they must also be *instructive*, have a certain cognitive value, and predict for us what is going to happen. These requirements leave one with the impression that truths of reason are truly extraordinary propositions: it is as if they were tautologies that managed to actually tell us things (without any risk of this content being disproved by future events), while at the same time being hypotheses that attain the status of tautologies (without being emptied of their instructive value with regard to the state of the world). But these two qualities are incompatible with each other. Take, for example, the principle of causality. If the proposition "everything that happens has a cause" is one that bears on the physical objects themselves, it must then be a hypothesis. But there must be some risk involved; the hypothesis cannot be held to be necessary: if it were, one would not even be able to conceive of what would have to happen for the hypothesis to be contradicted by experience. Yet if the principle is necessary, this means that experience is beside the point. Though instances of miracles—events that are disproportionate to anything that might have been their cause—are quite frequent, they do not lead us to reject the principle of causality (whose necessity we have posited). Rather they lead us to admit our own ignorance of the matter (i.e., we conclude that there is a cause, but that we are for the moment incapable of finding it).

Wittgenstein's well-known solution consists in pointing out the normative aspect of such truths of reason. According to him, they are like grammatical rules that must not be confused with propositions providing information about the world. In a lecture Wittgenstein once gave the following instructive example.[24] Having received two crates of apples, one containing twenty-five apples and the other sixteen, we put them all together in a big basket. Nobody touches them until they are

---

24. Ludwig Wittgenstein, *Wittgenstein's Lectures: Cambridge, 1932–1935*, ed. Alice Ambrose (Chicago: University of Chicago Press, 1982), p. 160.

counted again and we find there are only forty. An apple is missing. But the philosophical question here is: Why would an apple be missing? In reality, according to Wittgenstein, we have a "decision" to make, one that need not be made explicit, deliberated, or reflected upon. We either have to change our physics or our arithmetic. We will probably want to keep our arithmetic. Though we have to *make a decision* about this, we are not without reasons for preferring to maintain arithmetic (and logic) at the expense of physics. We therefore propose that "$25 + 16 = 41$" even if it has not proved to be (empirically) true. The above formula has become a *rule* that, along with other such formulas, determines the meaning of the activity of adding. If the result of an operation performed on 25 (apples) and 16 (apples) is not 41 (apples), then the operation is not what we call "addition." We therefore conclude that there are indeed forty-one apples, even if, physically, we only count forty. We will say that one apple may have been "lost," or that it has "disappeared" without our knowing how it happened. We have thereby modified our physics by introducing the possibility that apples can unaccountably disappear or that certain physical processes can take place without our knowing about them. As for arithmetic, it now takes on the status of a regulation governing the results of addition regardless of what actually happens, a rule that is thus in no wise meant to be a description of the state of the world, but rather a determination of the way we *want* to organize our thinking about the world. The other solution, one that is harder to imagine, would be to save our physics by changing our arithmetic: for example, we could use the previous operation "$+$" when counting sheep, dinner rolls, etcetera, and a new operation, say "$\blacklozenge$," which would be used for enumerating apples such that "$25 \blacklozenge 16 = 40$." The point of this example is that we have a choice when it comes to determining which *criterion* or rule of thought and expression to use. What is it that allows us to say that an apple is missing from the basket? One possible criterion is observation: we *saw* an apple leave the basket. Another is the arithmetical rule by which the expression "$25 + 16 = 41$" tells how many apples there are, when one adds them in quantities of 25 and 16. The arithmetical rule is not a description of reality. It is not an attempt to say how many apples are *in fact* in the basket; to know *that*, one has to go take a look. What the rule tells us is how to transform one expression in our language ("25 + 16") into an equivalent expression ("41"). Only after having adopted this system of representation can we consider such possibilities as an error in the count or an unexplained disappearance. The rule itself can be neither confirmed nor disproved by the observation of reality. It does not predict, with 100 percent probability, that the basket will contain forty-one apples. What it does is impose a form on the description of reality with regard to quantity. And *we* are the ones who provide the rule with this normative function: we make this rule into the criterion for what is, when nothing has been added or removed.

But here our language has brought us dangerously close to the territorial waters of legislative philosophy. It now seems as if *we* are the ones who decide what there is in the world. Our reason imposes whatever order it chooses on a reality that, in itself, is formless. We make things appear or disappear by means of dictates that have no other justification than that they satisfy our mode of representation. The rules of reasoning and calculation need not agree with reality. They are therefore *arbitrary*. At the very least they are *conventional*, and thus *artificial*. Consequently, we can easily imagine the convocation of a conference of metaphysicians (or of positivist antimetaphysicians) charged with the task of improving our language and forms of description. If we do not believe that philosophy can intervene in our language games in this way, we will have to conclude that philosophy has no further function to fulfill. Our language is arbitrary, and yet it is not *we* who construct it. This autonomous language is fatefully *imposed* on us. After following this line of thought to its conclusion, we realize that we have become *poststructuralists*.

The thesis according to which we are the ones who posit the rules we follow in our linguistic practice invariably provokes an astonished reaction. This is especially true if, like Wittgenstein, we include in linguistic practice not only the production of signs forming sentences, but also activities that have an internal relation to language such as counting, measuring, classing, arranging, using maps and diagrams, and so on. Some people might be concerned by this: if these activities have no ground, we will be reduced to relativism and sophistry. Others see just such sophistic themes underlying this view: everything is mere convention, artifice, and appearance. The view in question is that of the authors who are loosely grouped together under the label of "post-structuralism," and who share an obsession with dismantling a fanciful metaphysics that seems to them to be both firmly established and completely unbelievable. In the mid-nineteenth century, the first existentialists were convinced that reason, if left to its own devices, would come up with something like Hegel's System. Since they did not believe in this System, they were led to counter the Concept with Existence. What makes someone a poststructuralist is a fascination for a strain of French thought that has fallen prey to the "linguistic mirage."[25] French structuralism is only the most recent incarnation of the project of a unified science of everything, a "wissenschaftliche Weltauffassung." Structuralism, too, is in search of the "logical structure of the world." Yet its approach is governed by other authorities. A structuralist usually knows nothing about the Fregean renewal of logic: his paradigms come from linguistics, and he hopes to derive from them a *semiology* or a *semiotics*, a general theory of the laws of all representation (or of all communication of meaning using language). And structuralism also gives in to the temptation to draw up grandiose programs. "One day it will be demonstrated," says the structuralist, "that the structures of representation are those of the mind, that the structures of the mind are those of the brain, and finally, that the structures of the material system that is the brain are those of matter." Poststructuralism rejects this extravagant dogmatism. But its reaction is so vehement that it leads to a dogmatism which is just the reverse of that of the structuralist. Its thesis is that the world is not *order*, but *chaos*. What do we know about it? We only catch a glimpse of it in exceedingly rare moments of illumination or "laughter." The most frequently cited phrase from Foucault's book translated under the title *The Order of Things* is in fact a sentence by Borges that Foucault himself is citing: the tale of the (fictitious) Chinese encyclopedia whose classification seems absurd to us has the effect of a *koan*, a liberating paradox.[26]

---

25. See Thomas Pavel, *Le mirage linguistique* (Paris: Minuit, 1988). An English translation has been published under the title *The Feud of Language*, trans. Linda Jordan and Thomas G. Pavel (Oxford: Basil Blackwell, 1989).

26. Translator's note: In Borges's fictitious encyclopedia, "animals are divided into: (a) belonging to the Emperor, (b) embalmed, (c) tame, (d) sucking pigs, (e) sirens, (f)

What is absurd is not the system of classification of this particular encyclopedia, but the project of classification itself. Every order is arbitrary insofar as it never takes us outside of language and representation. Outside of language there is nothing to classify. It is not that there are no *things* outside of language but that they can only be classified in language or in the text. Here again the autonomy of grammar is upheld (or rather, the autonomy of language, for French structuralists have a purely lexical conception of language; the issue of the construction of the sentence never arises, for they see the sentence as another semiotic unity on a higher level than the word). But this thesis means that our concepts and classifications apply to the world of our representation and not to the thing in itself that is the world. Reality is fluid, continuous, and chaotic. But we cannot help but represent it as something stable, divided up into natural kinds, and orderly and regular in its functioning. We are constrained to represent the world as orderly, because that is the way a system of representation must "work." In short, it is impossible to represent the real; it preoccupies us, but only *in absentia*, by way of its "traces." It influences us only during moments of *ekstasis* when a situation arises that is excluded by the Western system of representation, leaving us dumbfounded and bewildered before the epiphany of the Other.

One might well conclude that poststructuralist philosophy has become captivated by a powerful image. Structuralism sometimes presents the diversity of human types using the image of a giant grid: each square is a human possibility, each culture occupies a square; in order to be human, one must be somewhere on the grid but one cannot be in more than one square; by *choosing* its square, a culture opts for certain possibilities of human life and excludes other such possibilities. This image is meant to show the common humanity of people who live in a wide variety of conditions. The image of a *choice* of certain cultural rules instead of others allows the anthropologist to situate himself before and *outside* of all cultures as a way

---

fabulous, (g) stray dogs, (h) included in the present classification, (i) frenzied, (j) innumerable, (k) drawn with a very fine camelhair brush, (l) *et cetera*, (m) having just broken the water pitcher, (n) that from a long way off look like flies." See Michel Foucault, *The Order of Things* (New York: Vintage, 1973), p. xv.

of explaining how communication *between* cultures is possible. Though we are on this square, we can understand the people on another square, because we *might have* chosen their rules rather than our own. This image is thus a way of saying that the difference between human types is not natural and cannot be explained by such things as climate and genetic makeup. A Huron Indian child raised in Paris will be a Parisian. Yet this image of cultural choice is *only* an image. False problems arise when one tries to build it into a hypothesis that would explain the hidden mechanism governing the formation of cultures. And the figure of the Philosopher-Legislator soon begins to loom on the horizon. For if we are to choose a culture, we must have reasons to prefer one culture over another. These reasons must be transcendental, given to us before we choose a square on the grid. Above all, they must not be taken from the rhetoric of our own current cultural position. Since he is nowhere on the board, the Legislator has no reason to choose one culture over another. He would be unable to apply any criteria for choice, inasmuch as his problem is precisely to make a decision in favor of the criteria of one culture over those of the others. The Legislator's decision is thus arbitrary. There is no cultural difference or table of values that is truly grounded. Everything is thus arbitrary.

Wittgenstein provides us with a means of escaping from the somewhat tiresome paradoxes of poststructuralism. Our language games may well be different in the sense that they are not imposed on us by a reality that it would be their task to reflect. But this does not mean that they have their origin in any real process of decision, whether one sees it as rational or irrational. In this regard, Jacques Bouveresse makes the following observation:

> Our language games and forms of life are not and cannot be "grounded" (a justification or a reason presupposes a language game within which justifications and reasons are provided and accepted). As a result, they also cannot be considered to be arbitrary, if by "arbitrary" one means that which should—and in other circumstances *could*—be justified, but which in the current situation is not.[27]

---

27. Bouveresse, "L'animal cérémoniel," pp. 68–69.

To say that language games are without a ground is thus misleading, if we understand this claim as a call to find the ground they lack, or, failing that, as a call to replace them with more rational games. Language games are not *lacking* a foundation just because they are without one. They escape the opposition between the justified and the unjustified, if the justification that one calls for is to be drawn from the nature of things (the nature of the universe or the nature of reason).

In a manuscript cited by Baker and Hacker, Wittgenstein writes:

> The rules of grammar are arbitrary means: their *purpose* is not (e.g.) to correspond to the essence of negation or colour—but is the purpose of negation and the concept of colour. As the purpose of the rules of chess is not to correspond to the essence of chess but to the purpose of the game of chess.
>
> Or: the rules of chess are not to correspond to the essence . . . of the chess king for they *give* it this essence, but the rules of cooking and roasting should indeed correspond to the nature of meat. This is, of course, a grammatical remark.[28]

By highlighting the difference between the rules of a game and those of the cooking of meat, this text serves to dispel the conceptual confusion sustained by themes like the arbitrariness of the linguistic sign or the conventional nature of all differences. The rules of chess create the difference between the *king* and the *queen* in a game of chess. The essence of the king is constituted by grammar, for a king is what the rules determine it will be. But the rules of cooking do not produce the difference between the *raw* and the *cooked*. This difference is in no way dependent on the mythology that subsequently *makes use* of it. In the case of chess, the game has no purpose external to itself and from which one could derive the set of its rules. One may choose to express this fact by saying that the rules are "groundless." The case of cooking is different: we do not *decide* that beef will have a different cooking time and taste than pork. What is more, even if we are free to cook our roast either in the oven or in a pot on the stove, we do not *decide* which of the two processes will make the meat juicier. The rules of

---

28. G. P. Baker and P. M. S. Hacker, *Wittgenstein: Grammar, Rules and Necessity* (Oxford: Basil Blackwell, 1985), p. 331.

cooking are dictated by a reality external to those rules: both the nature of meat and our own gastronomical requirements.

That grammar is autonomous means that the grammatical rules of thought need not justify themselves by some external purpose, as if the *telos* of thinking were to yield images of reality, and our task were to choose between ways of thinking as one chooses among different models of camera. Language is not a means that one would use for ends that could be conceived and articulated independently of language itself. As a result, if we meet someone who does not use the word "no" the way we do—that is, according to a rule by which "yes" and "no" are in contradiction with each other—we will not say that he is wrong or that he uses the word in a way that is forbidden by the essence of negation. But we will also not say that he has *discovered* a deeper meaning of negation or that he has understood its dialectical essence. We will certainly say that he is mistaken if he thinks that the new use that he has invented corresponds to our usual concept of negation. "There cannot be a question whether these or other rules are the correct ones for the use of 'not' (that is, whether they accord with its meaning). For without these rules the word has as yet no meaning; and if we change the rules, it now has another meaning (or none), and in that case we may just as well change the word too."[29] For Wittgenstein, grammar is as autonomous as the poststructuralist "signifier," but with none of the abyssal consequences that the poststructuralists have been somewhat quick to draw from their semiotic theoretical machine. Bouveresse provides the following summary of the meaning of the *invention of necessity* in Wittgenstein's thought: "We invent our concepts and create our grammar (under certain constraints and within certain limits). We obviously do not invent the reality that grammar allows us to describe and we do not create the truth that it allows us to recognize."[30]

Generally our institutions, languages, systems of classification, and calculating techniques are *groundless* because *we*—and not reality—

29. Ludwig Wittgenstein, *Philosophical Grammar*, ed. Rush Rhees, trans. Anthony Kenny (Berkeley: University of California Press, 1974), p. 184.

30. Jacques Bouveresse, *La force de la règle* (Paris: Minuit, 1987), p. 66.

decide what they will be. But the use of the word "decision" here may give rise to a misunderstanding. This term (rightfully) disquiets those for whom it has arbitrary resonances. This is what leads rationalists to construct epistemologies in which the rules to be followed are "grounded in reason." Empiricists, on the other hand, attempt to change these rules into linguistic conventions or innocuous tautologies. Nevertheless, such rival epistemologies have one thing in common: neither of them takes sufficient notice of the *normative* function of the principles of reason. Both of them seek to uncover a physical or mental deficiency, when what is really at issue in the principles of reason is the establishment—in advance of all factual observation—of what will be impossible as a matter of principle, so that expressions can then be endowed with meaning. The terms "yes" and "no" are opposed to each other only because we have excluded the possibility of the answer "yes and no," not because we have observed that reality does not admit of both responses at once. For reality can neither accept nor reject our responses until we have introduced the distinction between sense and non-sense.

The metaphor of "decision" should not be taken as anything other than a means of drawing attention to the difference between the way in which we justify (factual) truths and the way in which we justify (conceptual) decisions. Rom Harré explains this point well in a passage where he does not hesitate to avail himself of the distinction between *essence* and *accident*—a distinction denied by the implicit empiricism underlying most contemporary epistemologies—yet without assuming that there is any kind of *intuition* of the essences.

> Science is concerned with essences, not accidents. The taxonomic principles express the way in which it has come to be decided (and here we adopt the metaphor of "decision") that that distinction [between essences and accidents] will be made for that particular science. These are "decisions," not discoveries. They call for reasons in their justification, not for evidence.[31]

This latter distinction between the justification of decisions and the justification of discoveries leads us to another distinction, one that has

---

31. Rom Harré, *The Principles of Scientific Thinking* (Chicago: University of Chicago Press, 1970), p. 209.

been misunderstood by many philosophers: the distinction between practical rationality and theoretical rationality. It cannot be proved that a decision is just. If proofs can be provided as justification for a decision, it is not really a case of what we call a *decision*, but rather one of what we call a *discovery*. If we are only willing to recognize one sort of rationality, that of (empirical) discoveries, then we will be forced to say that decisions are irrational, inasmuch as they lack any foundation of the sort used in factual research. Yet one can still argue about decisions, bring the art of rhetoric to bear, and provide motives that make one decision preferable to another. The difference between decisions and discoveries is thus itself a product of philosophical grammar. Discoveries hinge on testimony, indices, marks of various kinds, regular observations, analogies, and inferences. When we do not know what they are based on, we call them *intuitions*. Decisions, on the other hand, have their "basis," to use Wittgenstein's terminology, in needs, desires, tastes, reasons of convenience, of utility, of opportunity. The notion of need should here be understood in the broadest sense: the needs that call for decisions may be material, spiritual, theoretical, collective, personal, and so on. When we do not know what a decision is based on, we say it is *arbitrary*.

These clarifications regarding the autonomy of rules suggest a way of avoiding the trap of the "problem of values." Underlying such "values" are *cultural categories*: the objective science of nature, the politics of the public good, the aesthetics of sensuous forms, the ethics of conscience, etcetera. It is not inappropriate to speak of "categories" here. For what they classify are the types of attribution, the broad kinds of questions that can be asked about a thing. And yet, the thing is not thereby to be thought in its "Being" (i.e., What is it? Where is it? What are its relations with other things? etc.). Rather, it is to be thought in its "value" or desirability.

For every object that we must evaluate in order to adopt a line of conduct toward it, there are several possible points of view. These points of view can be compared to the various opinions provided to a decision maker by his advisors. I will here call the decision maker "Free Will." Each advisor has a say in the matter from one and only one point of view. It is his job to *highlight* the point of view assigned to him, be it that of the costs and benefits of the operation, the political advantages and risks, the various amenities and the foreseeable difficulties, the juridical obstacles, or the possible objections of conscience. Though the deliberation will perhaps allow the project to be amended, there is no reason to expect that all of the various points of view can be reconciled. At the end of the deliberation, the Free Will passes judgment by saying *yes* or *no* to the thing proposed.

Now of all these advisors, one has a special role, and his opinion must necessarily be taken into account, without either restriction or correction, by the other advisors. This advisor is the one who explains the *physics* of the operation that the other advisors only consider from different points of view. The man of science describes how the operation will occur, should the Free Will decide to carry it out. Whether the project is good or bad considered from one perspective or another, it will always have this physical description. The scientific "point of view" is thus special: it is "objective" because it offers the only description of the thing that we must unconditionally accept, and against which we can bring no argument to bear. In this sense it is not a true "point of view." But at the same time this odd "point of view" is neutral: by itself, it provides no reason either for or against doing the thing in question. In other words, in our conception science is universal (it provides the *facts*) but abstract (it does not provide *values*).

The plurality of values allows the deliberation to be prolonged. In the end, it expands the powers of the Free Will, for he can always decide to hear from another advisor before concurring with those who have already spoken, even if they have been quite persuasive. Each advisor is expected to stay within his domain. Each of them is asked to say what should be done—what he himself would do—if there were only one order of considerations apt to provide us with motives for action. The advisor thus enjoys a kind of *autonomy*. He may develop all the consequences of a single set of reasons because he is not responsible for the final decision. As for the Free Will, he must decide the issue. In so doing, he also decides the respective weight of each of the various reasons presented in the case at hand.

The mystery of the function of the Free Will is thus that of the *jump* from a deliberation that has no internal reason to come to an end (only various *motives*: urgency, fatigue, etc.) to a decision that irrevocably ends the discussion. From a logical point of view, such a jump can be portrayed in the following way: as long as one is deliberating, the thing that one is discussing is considered in one or another of its aspects (i.e., *under a description*). It may be, for example, *politically* advantageous, but *economically* disastrous. We are thus in a realm ordered by adverbs. But as long as these adverbs are maintained, a restriction is placed on any conclusion. To say that the project is unsatisfactory from an economic point of view is to admit that there are other considerations that may be more important. The moment of decision is when the Free Will removes all the adverbs. If the proposed project is adopted, then it is simply good. If it is rejected, it is bad. The decision cannot retain the countless nuances of the deliberation. It cannot adopt the good points of the project while rejecting its bad ones (like those scrupulous voters who put several "yes" ballots and several "no" ballots into the same envelope, as a way of voicing in detail their opinion on the referendum at hand: *yes* to this consideration, *no* to that one, etc.).

The "problem of values" arises whenever one focuses on the fact that the passage from deliberation to decision entails a sovereign act that no "rational calculus" or "divine mathematics" or "principle of sufficient reason" can eliminate. At the same time that a Free Will decides whether or not to undertake a particular endeavor, he also decides (each time for the case at hand) an order of precedence among his advisors.

Thus, in the moment of deliberation, reason is divided into different legislations. Some philosophers like to stress what Kant called the "abysses" of reason.[32] Their philosophies, of what we might call "Levitical" inspiration, insist on the irreducibility of one category to another. One cannot derive the perspective of a different category through a deeper exploration of one's own. In order to reach the other interests of reason, one must leap. Indeed, Kant says that in order to bring out the difference between the "sensible" and the "super-sensible" (in our terms: between "facts" and "values"), one must act *as if* they were two "different worlds."[33] As we are well aware, the

---

32. Immanuel Kant, Introduction, *Critique of Judgment*, trans. Werner S. Pluhar (Indianapolis, Ind.: Hackett, 1987) §II.

33. Ibid.

entire philosophical problem here is that we are dealing with one and the same world. "The concept of freedom is to actualize in the world of sense the purpose enjoined by its laws."[34]

Philosophy thus takes as its task the organization of "passages" across the boundaries that have been so solemnly set up. It is then that another philosophy comes on the scene, one of what we might this time call a more "Hellenistic" inspiration. This philosophy finds "processions" and "mediations" wherever there are opposed terms. Among modern authors, Hegel's philosophy of Absolute Spirit is no doubt the best example of the refusal to *leap*: for him, art is already religion and religion, though it of course maintains an "artistic" moment, already prefigures the content of the philosophical concept.

Unlike categories of Being, which, because the concept of being is not generic, form an ultimate organization, the categories of human action cannot represent such an ultimate organization. If there is any sense to deliberating before taking action, the categorical perspectives from which value judgments are successively made must not be unconnected. We only behave *as if* they were unconnected for the purposes of deliberation.[35]

It is here that the Wittgensteinian distinction proposed earlier may be of some help. Whatever they may have claimed, the thinkers of the seventeenth century did not *discover* that values existed in the subject's judgment rather than in the world. The human mind did not suddenly emerge from a longstanding confusion between the thing considered in itself (figure and movement and, for some people, force) and the thing considered in relation to our needs and fantasies (colors, flavors, pleasure, etc.). Rather, the thinkers of the seventeenth century *decided* (for reasons that are of the order of motives and not that of proofs) that henceforth only things taken outside of every human context—

---

34. Ibid.

35. In the preceding sentences, the words "cannot" and "must" are statements about philosophers, not about the nature of things. They should not be seen as a "transcendental argument," but as a reminder of a trivial but incontestable fact: practical rationality is part of a *deliberation* (one that, for the philosopher, corresponds to the "division of reason") which is supposed to culminate in a *decision* to either take or not take action (a decision that reintroduces the "unity of reason").

without consideration of the needs, labors, drives, scruples, and face-tiousness of man—will be held to be real. This decision has long been portrayed by the epic histories of the evolution of the human mind as a discovery. But how could it be discovered that there are no values in the world, only "things" or "facts"? How could it be determined? Where would one look? Moreover, at any time we are liable to return to the premodern mode of representation of a world abounding with values: Is it not a fact that some climates are inhospitable and others calm, that some mushrooms are edible and others poisonous, that some lines of reasoning are valid and others invalid? The error of evolutionists, in anthropology as in the history of ideas, is to attempt to represent the *institution* of new categories of thought as *progress*. I am prepared to follow Castoriadis in calling this institution "imagi-nary," as long as this term is stripped of any nocturnal connotations and retains only those of ingenuity and inventiveness. The divisions of reason were not always there, present in the transcendental structure of rationality and waiting to be brought to light by the penetrating insight of some philosopher. It is true that these divisions were locally anticipated in the form of those *distinguo* that are worked out in the course of discussions. What was lacking was the *idea* (or the force of imagination) to generalize such possible discussions and establish them *as if* they corresponded to breaches opened within the very es-sence of reason.

Now what has just been said regarding the difference between fact (the degree zero of value) and value is also applicable to the differences between values. The thinkers of the sixteenth century did not discover that until that time the essence of the religious and the essence of the political had been confused with each other, although they were in fact distinct. The only thing they discovered was that one could make this distinction. That is why, in an age plagued by wars of religion, they decided that this distinction should be made. Historians are concerned with the circumstances in which it became normal to draw a distinc-tion between truths of science and truths of revelation, between the Prince and conscience, between political good and universal good, between Church and State, between morality and fiction, and so on. My topic, however, is not this history, but the philosophical difficulty that arises when one notices that the array of practical categories is justified (it has, as Wittgenstein would say, a "basis") but cannot be provided with an ultimate ground.

Each time that a practical category is distinguished, it takes on an autonomy by which it is freed from the constraints of higher purposes. The proper word for this is "absolutism," for here a human end or purpose (one possible motive for action among others) is detached from a previously given order of all such ends. The absolutist Prince is subject to no law, he is *legibus solutus,* his will is neither held in check by a superior Order of things nor subject to any worldly justice whatever. But each conceivable category defines a different absolute: in addition to the political absolute ("politics first!" = first the national good), there is the possibility of a moral absolute ("truth and justice, whatever the cost"), a *literary absolute,*[36] etcetera. Thus, though the elevation of a particular point of view into a "value" should be understood as a restriction, it invariably leads to the temptation to give this point of view unlimited compass. It is the duty of the Statesman to watch over public issues and to attend to the public good that the various factions lose sight of in the course of their conflicts; this means that he must not interfere with the conscience of political subjects. Yet the formation of a *restricted absolute* is so unnatural that it takes centuries even to become established in one way or another. The restricted absolute is constantly mistaken for the absolute *tout court.*

This is why, in a culture organized around something like a generalized Free Will, some have felt the need to insist on the *self-limitation* of the sovereign will (Castoriadis) or the *hierarchy* of ends (Dumont). These terms designate results that cannot be brought about through a proclamation or political act: only an *education* in the restriction of the absolute can set up the sort of "basis" that would provide justifications for our institutions. As for the content of such restriction, it can be reduced to this: whoever speaks in the name of an established

---

36. See the book by Philippe Lacoue-Labarthe and Jean-Luc Nancy that bears this title: *L'absolu littéraire* (Paris: Seuil, 1978); a partial English translation is available as *The Literary Absolute: The Theory of Literature in German Romanticism,* trans. Philip Barnard and Cheryl Lester (Albany: State University of New York Press, 1988).

category and takes pride in being its *pure* representative (a pure scholar, a pure artist, etc.) must understand that he no longer speaks in the name of all the categories. The philosopher's position, however, is more delicate. We expect the philosopher to maintain for us the view of the whole: we call on him to delineate the limits of each of the particular points of view. But why should this be so difficult to do without lapsing into pomposity? The reason is that there are two ways of carrying out the assignment: one can do so from a position either *before* or *after* the division of "modern reason" into practical categories made absolute within their order (but only within their order).

To take a position downstream from the separation of the waters of reason into different tributaries is to seek to limit the claims of each point of view by devising a *synthesis*. Yet such a synthesis must start somewhere. The philosopher cannot avoid taking up one of the practical categories and attempting to expand its horizons. This way of doing things is condemned in advance, for the relevance of each specialty is a result of its restricted competence.

Teilhard de Chardin once explained that he was not a practitioner of metaphysics—a scholastic and old-fashioned field—but of *hyperphysics*. A hyperphysics would be a truly stupendous discipline: it would be scientific like our physics (which, taken in our sense of the word, strives to provide a description of a world devoid of "human phenomena"), and at the same time would offer a view of the whole (yielding the description of a world at the center of which are "human phenomena").

The punishment for all the speculative exertions that position themselves downstream from the modern division of the rational is to share the fate of hyperphysics. Each of them is afflicted with a malady that destroys both style and thought: grandiloquence.[37] They end up in a kind of scientistic superscience, or *gnosis*, unless of course they favor the *hyperpolitics* of terroristic thinkers or the *hyperaesthetics* of dilettantes.

But how are we to go about placing ourselves *upstream* from the division of rationality into different points of view? The significance of the current return to Kant perhaps lies in this question. It is hoped that

---

37. See Clément Rosset's comments on grandiloquent style as indicative of a poverty of thought in *Le réel* (Paris: Minuit, 1977).

Kant will provide a way for us to accept the division of reason, and will do so by means of reasons drawn from a deeper, more original unity rather than from some synthetically derived one. Still, Kant's name has become somewhat legendary in the course of the debate. Indeed, the "Kant" we might invoke in this case is a Kant disengaged from the main tenets of Kantianism. It would be Kant minus the principle of causality, for this principle combines the difficulties of the empiricist (who reduces causality to a regular conjunction within our observations) with those of the rationalist (who converts natural causality into a logical link of the form: *if . . . then*). It would also be a Kant without the categorical imperative (which does not tell us enough if it is drawn from pure reason, but cannot be drawn from pure reason if it is to guide us).

A reference to Kant on my part would therefore be either misleading or empty. That is why I prefer to make use of one of Baudelaire's remarks in order to elucidate the logic of our value judgments. In his article on Flaubert, Baudelaire reproaches those critics who condemned *Madame Bovary* for having "mixed genres." These critics complained that there was no character in the novel who could be held to represent public morality and the conscience of the author. Baudelaire responds that the place of such a character is not within the limits of this novel. The work must obey its own laws. By insisting that the novelist set a moral example, these critics make literature *absolute* in the wrong way: they change the author into a sort of guiding conscience. Yet the author cannot be such a conscience, if he has accepted the dictates of modern art. And anyway, if we lived in a theocracy, why would we look to poets and novelists to be our guides? Baudelaire shows how the literary absolute is only conceivable within *limits*. The pure artist will not allow himself to transgress these limits from which he derives all his (literary) freedom, but only because he assumes that the freedom of his readers is still more radical.

> Where, oh! where is the proverbial and legendary character whose job it is to explain the fable and guide the reader's understanding? In other words, where is the accusing finger?
> Rubbish! An eternal and incorrigible confusion of functions and genres! —A true work of art has no need of an indictment. The

logic of the work itself is equal to all the postulates of morality, and it is up to the reader to draw the conclusions from the conclusion.[38]

The philosopher is tempted to generalize this last point. Wherever an "absolute" is instituted, there results a logic that imposes a conclusion within the limits of the work. Those who serve this absolute know that they can fully give in to the logic of the work, precisely because it is partial. The requirements of morality do not dictate that an indictment be included in the work. Rather, they impose the exclusion of indictments. For it is the reader's job to draw *the conclusions from the conclusion.*

---

38. Baudelaire, "*Madame Bovary* by Gustave Flaubert," in *Selected Writings on Art and Artists*, trans. P. E. Charvet (Cambridge: Cambridge University Press, 1972), p. 250.

Name Index

Subject Index